THE CANADA AND HAMILTON CLOCK COMPANIES

Frontispiece: This "Simpson" timepiece by the Hamilton Clock Co. honoured the company president — over a century ago.

THE CANADA AND HAMILTON
CLOCK COMPANIES

by

Jane Varkaris & James E. Connell

THE BOSTON MILLS PRESS

Canadian Cataloguing in Publication Data

Varkaris, Jane, 1928-
    The Canada and Hamilton Clock Companies

Bibliography: p.
ISBN 0-919783-21-X

1. Canada Clock Company - History. 2. Clock and watch makers - Ontario. 3. Clock and watch making - Ontario - History. I. Connell, James E. II. Title.

TS543.C2V37 1986   338.7'681113   C86-093797-6

© Jane Varkaris and James E. Connell, 1986

Edited by Noel Hudson
Designed by John Denison
Cover Design by Gill Stead
Cover Photos by G.W. Campbell
Typeset by Speed River Graphics
Printed by Ampersand, Guelph

Published by:
THE BOSTON MILLS PRESS
132 Main Street
Erin, Ontario N0B 1T0

We wish to acknowledge the financial assistance and encouragement of The Canada Council, the Ontario Arts Council and the Office of the Secretary of State.

FOREWORD

The Canada Clock Company was established just five years after the Dominion of Canada was formed. They ceased business before Arthur Pequegnat started manufacturing clocks. Although in business only a few years, they were an important cog in the wheels of time for Canadian industry in general and clock manufacturing in particular.

In this book, Jim Connell and Jane Varkaris present proof that the Canada Clock Company and the Hamilton Clock Company actually manufactured both cases and movements in Canada. They have with this book thereby given us one more reason to be justly proud of our forefathers' accomplishments in this fine country of ours.

Clock collectors everywhere owe a great debt of gratitude to the authors for this comprehensive work that obviously required many diligent hours of hard work and a great amount of dedication.

G. Edmond Burrows

ACKNOWLEDGEMENTS

Many persons contributed generously to the completion of this book. We owe a special debt of gratitude to Dr. Snowden Taylor, whose advice and assistance greatly aided our study of the clock movements and their origins. We wish to thank Costas Varkaris and Cathie Varkaris for help in preparing the manuscript, and Marilyn Connell for many favours, especially her eagle-eyed correction of proofs. Thanks, too, to Harold McNutt for assistance with photography.

A special acknowledgement must also be made to Stan and Vivien Herzog. They became interested in the Canada and Hamilton Clock Companies during the early 1970s. After several years of research, they compiled an impressive amount of information. Unfortunately, due to other pressures and interests, the work was never completed. Mr. and Mrs. Herzog generously offered the results of their labours to the authors of this book. There was duplication, to be sure, but this was reassuring, since it provided confirmation from another source. They were able to contribute illustrations and data which otherwise would now have been unobtainable. Their support was most welcome.

We wish to express our thanks and appreciation to the following persons who furnished information, provided pictures and allowed the authors to photograph their clocks: W. Grant Allen, Harvey K. Andreasen, Donalda Badone, Ray Benben, Peter Betts, John Burke, G. Edmond Burrows, J.W. Chisholm, George Chopping, James Christian III, E.J. Collins, Robert Connell, Bruce Cook, Mel Dowdall, Duane Fitchet, Fred Foster, Ken Fram, Gord Gibbins, Jim Halls, Irene & George Hartwick, Owen Hawkins, John Haze, Patrick Hobson, Bryan Hollebone, Martin H. Howard, Paul & Sharon Johnston, Sarah Kapitan, Paul Lavoie, T. Wm. Lawler, Maurice Le Clair, Harold Leach, Michael Mazur, Reid Matheson, Burt Miller, Jim Miller, Paul Morgan, Mr. MacLean, RoseAnn Newman, Earl Pascoe, Robert Phillip, J. Plewes, Harry Porter, A.M. Provick, Russell Riguse, John Ruhland, Roy Sennett, Scott Silmser, Allan Symons, Rick Taylor, George Werden, Brian Winter, Aaron Wohl.

TABLE OF CONTENTS

Fig. 1 THE MUSIC HALL
Previously the Canada Clock Company Factory
From the Illustrated Historical Atlas of the County of Ontario, 1877.

PART I: THE COMPANIES

CHAPTER ONE
CANADA CLOCK COMPANY, WHITBY, ONTARIO

In the spring of 1872, Canada's first clock factory, the Canada Clock Company, was established in Whitby. Whitby is a county town that was incorporated in 1855 and is located 19 miles east of Toronto, Ontario.

From records gathered by the Whitby Historical Society and Stan and Vivien Herzog, it was concluded that this company was formed by William F. Collins and his brothers, John F. and Edward. In March 1872, the brothers applied to the Town Council of Whitby for permission to erect a steam engine of 10 horsepower for manufacturing purposes. On 21 March, on a motion by Mr. Powell, "leave was granted Messrs. Collins Bros." to erect the engine.

From June to December, John F. Collins and his brothers carried out the all-important task of equipping the factory. John F., who apparently had mechanical and clockmaking experience, was the manager.

The factory was located on the southeast corner of Brock Street and Colborne Street. A description of the building and its contents was located in an article in the *Whitby Chronicle* of 6 March 1873, quoted below:

At first sight one cannot fail to be struck with the relative insignificance of the building compared with the large amount of costly machinery which it contains. The building is two stories, 100x50 feet. The first floor is the general workshop and contains all the heavy machinery. Entering it, attention is arrested by the busy hum and whirl of complicated machinery. To the left are three costly turning lathes used in making punches, stamps and dies; a large arched adjustable press for punching and heavy work of the kind, and weighing some thirty hundred-weight; a friction drop press, a single action press, the latter calculated for manipulating the finer work. We next come to a wheelcutter, a beautifully finished machine costing alone $1,200 and with a capacity of cutting the cogs in ten thousand wheels a day. This machine makes no less that 4,400 revolutions in a minute. Further on there are three of what are called chuck lathes, applied to turning and finishing pinions, centre shafts, etc. Turning round we encounter a machine for drilling pinions, revolving with lightning speed, making, we are told, sixteen thousand revolutions per minute and capable of turning out work enough for fifteen thousand clocks a month. So delicately constructed is this machine and so finely adjusted that the turning of one cog removes a plate the thousandth part of an inch! Next we were introduced to a ratchet cutter, going with similar velocity and capable of executing an equal amount of work in a given time. The dial plate of this machine is so constructed as to cut any desired number — from six to twenty four teeth at a time in every ratchet. The movement of this seems like perfection itself, and withal so simple that it can be raised and lowered at pleasure by touching a screw at the top of the bed. It was making at a rate of four thousand revolutions a minute. A vertical drill is the next object of attention. It is used for drilling and counter-boring all kinds of small work, also for shaving the tops of brass, for what is called "bushing," reassembling (sic) the jewelled holes in watches.

In the addition or lean-to, the building on the west side are the wire rollers and also the chemical apparatus for brightening the works. There is also a blacksmith's shop with regular forge; and another compartment containing the boiler from which the engine is served. There are likewise several labour-saving contrivances for pumping water and keeping a never-failing stream flowing through the factory. The engine is an excellent one (we did not learn how many horse power) manufactured at the Joseph Hall Works, Oshawa, and there are altogether in use upwards of eighty feet of shafting.

Returning through the general workshop we have pointed out to us machines for straightening out coiled wire, rollers for flattening and rolling pendulum wires, etc., also an emery wheel for brightening the works — four vices and benches at which workmen are engaged, and various other contrivances — as the auctioneer says in the bills — too numerous to mention.

The upper storey contains four departments — one for case work — one for veneering and varnishing, a third for polishing and finishing, and a well lighted airy room called the movement room for putting the works together. We were shown the quality of the wood used, and had an opportunity of comparing it with that used in American clocks and the contrast was indeed remarkable. The quality of the latter could not for one moment compare with the beautiful wood introduced into their clock cases by Messrs. Collins.

We next descended to the shipping room — encountering on the way a buffing wheel used for preparing the veneering — and here seated we noted the following figures, given us in reply to questions put to the managing partner of the firm. Value of machinery and plant, about $20,000; quantity of brass used per month, about $5,000; wire, $500; wood, $1,500; veneer, $1,000; varnish, $150. Stock on hand ready for shipment, to the value of about $12,000, capacity for work, about five thousand clocks per month.

The Messrs. Collins commenced the work in June last; they now employ some fifteen hands and with enlarged premises (which they very much require) could employ from fifty to one hundred men, should their enterprise prove a success. Of the latter they have full confidence. They possess the only clock factory in the Dominion and the quality of their work is acknowledged to be much superior — while the price is lower — than the clocks turned out by similar establishments in the United States.

In concluding our hurried description it is only necessary to add that Messrs. Collins with the costly machinery they possess, can make any style of clock — spring, alarm, or regulator, or anything else required — 'To measure old time as it goes' — and they can also turn out almost anything required to be made in brass. Here is another chance for Whitby men who want to encourage manufacturers.

In this factory, the first clock was manufactured in mid-January 1873. By August of that year, William F. Collins believed that it was necessary to refinance the company. He, with a group of Port Hope men, decided to incorporate and indicated their intention in the *Canada Gazette* to apply for letters patent. (See Appendix 3)

However, before an application was made, it appears that John Hamer Greenwood decided to purchase the company and became its principal investor. He was, at that time, Mayor of Whitby and one of the reasons for his action was, no doubt, the desire to keep this industry in Whitby.

Labels of the clocks manufactured by the Canada Clock Company now began to carry the names of J. Hamer Greenwood, president, and John F. Collins, manager. According to the *Whitby Chronicle*, the company was somewhat successful and, by the fall of 1874, substantial orders were shipped to Berlin, Ontario, and Montreal, Quebec. Unfortunately, by early 1875, due to the "human failings" of President Greenwood, who had become insolvent, the factory was listed as one of his assets to be disposed of by his creditors. In March 1875, a meeting of the creditors was held at the clock factory, where they discussed the disposition of President Greenwood's assets; the factory was valued at $46,000.

In April 1875, Colonel James Wallace became the owner of the factory, hoping to make the clock company a profitable enterprise. Carloads of clocks were shipped from the factory, some destined for the Grand Trunk Railway Company. In the ensuing months, however, the profitability status of the operations became questionable. The *Whitby Chronicle* commented more than once on the need for additional capital.

In order to help ensure the success of the company, diversification was introduced in June 1875. The company began manufacturing an instrument considered to be a "lock timer device." The instrument was designed by Mr. Hennessy, a lock and safe maker of Hamilton, and was patented in Ottawa and Washington. The instrument had a spring, was wound up like a clock and ran for a maximum of 60 hours. The company received an order for 500 such instruments and hoped for additional orders; however, no additional orders were ever received.

By October 1875, the company moved into the export market and orders were received from Edinburgh, Scotland. This sale provided Col. Wallace with hopes that the British market might absorb two thirds of the firm's annual production, estimated at $50,000-$60,000 worth of clocks. A lucrative export market was the only hope for the company to become profitable and stay in production. In spite of Col. Wallace's optimism and predictions by the *Ontario Reformer* that the company was "becoming a prosperous concern," on the third week of October 1875, Col. Wallace held a meeting with a view to disposing of the company's assets.

On 22 October 1875, the meeting took place at the Commercial Hotel in Oshawa. Persons interested in the manufacture of clocks were invited. The *Ontario Reformer* in Oshawa reported:

On Monday last a large number of our citizens met Col. Wallace of Whitby and purchased the plant and stock of the Whitby Clock Factory. The sum of $15,000 capital has been raised and the building known as the old Christian Church secured in which to carry on the business of clock making. We wish the new business every success.

Although it was assumed that the purchase was completed, in the ensuing three weeks the arrangements did not go well and the deal did not materialize. Col. Wallace looked elsewhere for buyers, and on November 24, 1875, the *Oshawa Vindicator* reported:

The proprietor of the Clock Factory whose negotiations with Oshawa fell through a short time ago is now arranging to send the establishment to Port Hope. A deputation of the Port Hope Board of Trade visited Whitby a short time ago and examined the establishment. Port Hope is asked to raise $20,000 of stock.

Apparently, the deal was unsuccessful and the Port Hope Board of Trade met with Col. Wallace to ask him for an explanation. The *Oshawa Vindicator* reported on the meeting in its December 1, 1875, issue as follows:

Here is the explanation given to the Port Hope Board of Trade by Col. Wallace why he did not come to Oshawa with the clock factory as reported in the papers.
"Three gentlemen there had taken an active part in getting up a company and

had agreed to take $1,000 each in stock. A building was bought and everything ready to complete arrangements with Mr. Wallace. But when such was to be done, these three men said they had taken such an active part in organizing the company they ought to have the thousand dollars stock each given to them. He could not see it in the same light as they and the matter dropped there, leaving the contemplated company with a building on their hands." This is a nice story to be sure. Who were they Col. Wallace?

On 2 December 1875, all negotiations came to an abrupt end. About 6:50 p.m. a fire started and quickly spread through the roof and upper floor of the factory. Although the factory and its contents were insured, the insured value was about one quarter of the actual worth. Consequently, The Phoenix, Royal and Western Insurance Companies paid about $10,000.

Sometime during the period in which he was in charge of the factory, Wallace imported movements from the Ansonia Clock Company in Connecticut, U.S.A. It is not known whether these movements were brought into Whitby when Wallace decided that the factory could not be operated profitably or whether they were imported after the fire. It is known that many cases were in existence after the movement-making operations had stopped and that Wallace, in order to cut his losses, fitted the cases with Ansonia movements.

In May 1876, Col. Wallace sold the equipment to a new clock company which was starting in Hamilton and organized a public auction to take place on July 19, 1876, to dispose of a number of factory items. Col. Wallace appointed Mr. L. Fairbanks as the auctioneer, and among the items he offered for auction were: five hundred 30-hour OG weight strike clocks; one hundred 8-day "Octagon Prize" spring striking clocks; one hundred and twenty 30-hour "Octagon Prize" clocks; eighty-five 30-hour and 8-day cottage clocks; and twenty regulators. (For more details of items auctioned, see Appendix 1.)

The auction apparently was not very successful, because about a year later, May 22, 1877, an advertisement appeared in the *Whitby Chronicle* advertising many of the same items as in the auction of July 1876. (See Appendix 2)

In November 1876, the building that housed the clock factory was sold to Mr. G. Hopkins for $7,500. Mr. Hopkins converted the upper storey into a "Music Hall" in 1877 and intended to use the lower storey for stores. The picture of the Music Hall, however, does not show any stores on the first floor. The building in 1879 became the "Whitby Town Hall" and remained as such until its demolition in 1960. The site is now the location of the firehall.

CHAPTER TWO
HAMILTON CLOCK COMPANY, HAMILTON, ONTARIO

With the failure of the Canada Clock Company in Whitby, a new company was formed in Hamilton in 1876 by James Simpson and George Lee. They invited John F. Collins to move from Whitby to join them as the manager due to his expertise in the clockmaking business. The company, which was established with a capital of $100,000, was named "Hamilton Clock Company" and the factory location was on the corner of Cathcart Street and Kelly Street in the City of Hamilton, Ontario. The building had previously housed the Hespeler Sewing Machine Company. The newly formed company was given a chance to become profitable by the City Council of Hamilton. A letter written by the Finance Committee to Mayor and Aldermen on 27 May 1876 proposed that, with the exception of the land occupied by the building and the water rate, the taxes of the Hamilton Clock Company be exempt for a period of five years.

John F. Collins moved to Hamilton and lived with his parents and brother, Edward. His father had a veterinary practice in the city. Shortly after John moved to Hamilton, his brother, Edward, joined him for a short time as a clock finisher at the Hamilton Clock Company.

The *Hamilton Directory* of 1877, which lists John F. Collins as being associated with the newly formed Hamilton Clock Company, also lists at least six men as clockmakers in the same year. The names include Alexander Grant, Richard Martin, Charles Lammas, Orlando Carroll, Joseph Brown and Addison Smith. Several men were listed as "clockmakers" in one year only. None appeared as clockmakers beyond the 1878-79 city directory. Alexander Grant's name was again in the 1884-85 directory as clockmaker and Irving Franklin was clockmaker in the 1885-86 directory. Although no record was found linking these men to the Hamilton Clock Company, the presence of clockmakers in the year that the clock factory opened is no doubt significant.

James Simpson, who was a wholesale grocer, became the president of the company and George Lee, a fruit, game and oyster dealer and restaurateur, was appointed the business manager.

Although associated with the Hamilton Clock Company for a number of years, John F. Collins apparently had an altercation with George Lee and James Simpson. The court, asked to solve their differences in February 1879, decided in favour of the defendants and against the plaintiff, John F. Collins. Collins left the company about this time. A few labels have been seen with the names of Lee and Simpson only. They may well date from the 1879-1880 period.

The name of the company listed in directories and frequently stamped on the movements of the clocks was "Hamilton Clock Co." The company also used the traditional label affixed to the clock case to identify its products. The name appears in engravings of the factory, illustrated on many of these labels. Occasionally, elsewhere on the label, the company is referred to as the "Hamilton Clock Manufacturing Co."

Although no records are available showing when the company ceased operations, the authors believe that the company went out of business around 1880. This belief is based on information concerning the Canada Clock Company, Ltd., Hamilton, Ontario.

Fig. 2. *Factory of the Hamilton Clock Company*
From Label Engraving.

Fig. 3. *After 1880, the Canada Clock Company Ltd. continued*
to use the same engraving as its predecessor (Fig. 2) with name change.

CHAPTER THREE
CANADA CLOCK COMPANY LTD., HAMILTON, ONTARIO

When the Hamilton Clock Company ceased operation, James Simpson was anxious to form a new company and to resume manufacturing clocks. With several Hamilton businessmen, a new company called the Canada Clock Company Ltd. was formed in late 1880 and clocks were manufactured in the same building occupied previously by the Hamilton Clock Company, at 26-28 Cathcart Street. The 1880 *Province of Ontario Directory* listed James Simpson as president and Adam Rutherford as manager of the new company. In addition, beginning in 1883, John M. Lester's name appeared as the secretary-treasurer.

As in 1876, a committee approached the Hamilton City Council in December 1880 asking that the building, machinery, plant and personal property of the company be exempt from taxation for a period not exceeding seven years and beginning on 1 January 1881.

The original letters patent still exists incorporating the Canada Clock Company (Limited) and is held on file by the government. The letters patent is dated 28 February 1881 and was recorded on 16 March 1881. The document provides an interesting insight into the company and is reproduced in part on the following page. (See Fig. 4) According to this document, John F. Collins was not involved in this new company. The 1881 census listed Collins as a jeweller, and within a few years he had moved to Toronto and into another business.

As indicated by the document, the capital stock of the Canada Clock Company Ltd. was $50,000, divided into five hundred shares of $100 each. The shares were divided among the participating men as listed in the letters patent. James Simpson, Adam Rutherford and Edmund Scheuer were first or provisional company directors.

The journal *The Canadian Manufacturer*, 19 October 1883, in a section on Hamilton industries, quoted the *Evening Tribune* article titled, "The Canada Clock Company's Works":

> It may be news to the many residents of the "Ambitious City" to learn that the Canada Clock Company, whose factory is situated on the corner of Cathcart and Kelly streets, are the only manufacturers of clocks in this broad Dominion. Such, however, is the case, and of course no more suitable place could have been found for such an establishment than this fair city. It is marvellous to take a walk through the various departments in the factory and see to what perfection machinery has been brought, when the delicate works comprising the interior of a clock can all be cut out and shaped by machines with an accuracy which could not possibly be arrived at — except with excessive labor and great loss of time — with tools in the hands of workmen. As it is, however, nothing is thought of turning out from two to five thousand clocks of the same size and pattern in which there will not be the slightest flaw or the slightest difference in detail. A good deal of work, indeed, is done by mere youths, the machinery taking the

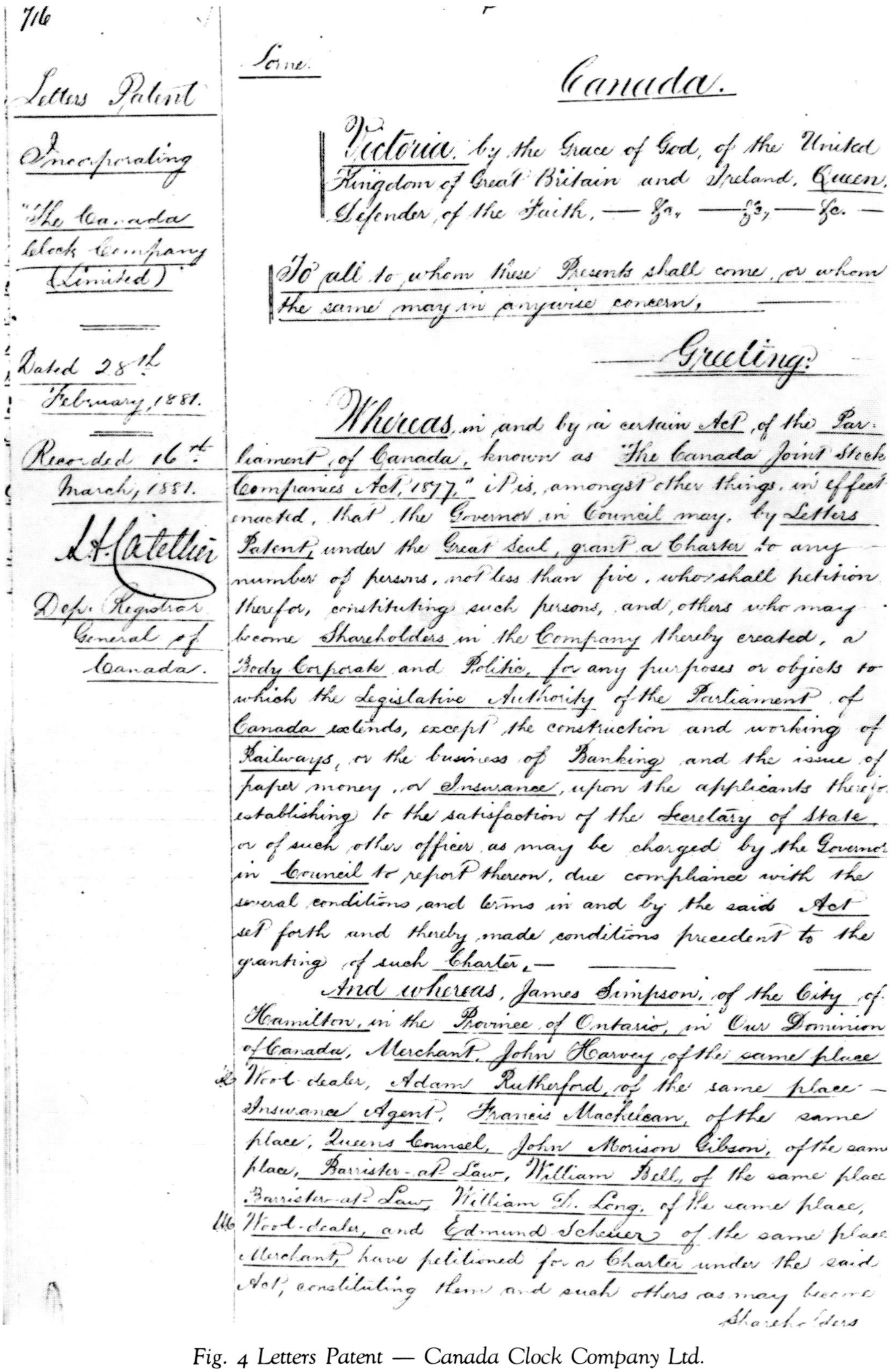

716

Letters Patent

Incorporating

"The Canada
Clock Company
(Limited)

Dated 28th
February, 1881.

Recorded 16th
March, 1881.

J.H. Catellier

Dep. Registrar
General of
Canada.

Seine

Canada.

Victoria, by the Grace of God, of the United
Kingdom of Great Britain and Ireland, Queen,
Defender of the Faith, — &c., — &c, — &c. —

To all to whom these Presents shall come, or whom
the same may in anywise concern, —

Greeting: —

Whereas, in and by a certain Act, of the Parliament, of Canada, known as "The Canada Joint Stock
Companies Act, 1877," it is, amongst other things, in effect
enacted, that the Governor in Council may, by Letters
Patent, under the Great Seal, grant a Charter to any
number of persons, not less than five, who shall petition
therefor, constituting such persons, and, others who may
become Shareholders in the Company thereby created, a
Body Corporate and Politic, for any purposes or objects to
which the Legislative Authority of the Parliament, of
Canada extends, except the construction and working of
Railways, or the business of Banking, and the issue of
paper money, or Insurance, upon the applicants thereof
establishing to the satisfaction of the Secretary of State,
or of such other officer, as may be charged by the Governor
in Council to report thereon, due compliance with the
several conditions, and terms in and by the said Act
set forth and thereby made conditions precedent to the
granting of such Charter, —

And whereas, James Simpson, of the City, of
Hamilton, in the Province of Ontario, in Our Dominion
of Canada, Merchant, John Harvey of the same place
Wool dealer, Adam Rutherford, of the same place —
Insurance Agent, Francis Mackelcan, of the same
place, Queens Counsel, John Morison Gibson, of the same
place, Barrister-at-Law, William Bell, of the same place
Barrister-at-Law, William J. Long, of the same place,
Wool dealer, and Edmund Scheuer of the same place
Merchant, have petitioned for a Charter under the said
Act, constituting them and such others as may become
Shareholders

Fig. 4 Letters Patent — Canada Clock Company Ltd.
from the Ministry of Consumer and Commercial Relations,
Government of Ontario.

part — and taking it well — of skilled mechanics. "I presume," said the reporter to the manager of the company, "your hands are mostly Americans, as I do not suppose you could find Canadians skilled in this branch of industry." "On the contrary," replied the manager, "out of fifty hands employed by us we have only two Americans. We find the youth of the neighboring villages very apt at learning how to run our machinery, and we have no need to look abroad for help. Our hands," he continued, "seem to take an interest in their work. They know everything must be done just so and should a fault in any piece be detected, the foreman knows at once where to place the blame. This, together with the fact that the majority of the well meaning young men in any branch of manufacturing do not wish a fault to be found with work which has passed through their hands, secures us an absolute degree of accuracy even in the most intricate parts of our clock movements."

HOW CLOCKS ARE MADE

It may be said that, with the exception of the springs, everything connected with these clocks is manufactured on the premises. This has only, to a great extent, been obtained since the N.P. came into existence, its preventive tariff of 35 percent, shutting out the American Manufacturers from sending the "interior economy" of the clocks — so to speak — across the line. *(Author's Note: The N.P. referred to above was the "National Policy" of Sir John A. Macdonald. Macdonald was re-elected as Prime Minister in 1878 after promising to encourage Canadian manufacturing by means of protective tariffs. No doubt the National Policy encouraged the revitalization of the Canada Clock Company, which took place in 1881.)* The brass, however, with which the works are made is still imported from the United States, but the day is not far distant, at least so the reporter was informed, when that very necessary article will also become one of Hamilton's industries. In the machinery room the brass is cut into sizes for the various parts of the movements. Then the plates which hold the parts together are shaped by a punching machine, which makes a correct plate each time it descends. Here, also, the wheels and pinions are made by ingenious machinery, which is driven at a high rate of speed, one turning lathe being driven at the extraordinarily high speed of 9000 revolutions per minute. In fact it revolves so rapidly that to the reporter it seemed as thought it were standing perfectly still till he attempted to touch it with his fingers, when he discovered it was rapidly revolving. The pinion drilling machine and the wheel cutter are looked after by one man, and as on these parts being perfect depends the accuracy of the movement, the greatest care has to be taken that the holes made in the pinions and the teeth in the wheels are cut out at exactly the same distance from each other. This could hardly be accomplished with any degree of success except by machinery, but the foreman assured the reporter that it was a rare thing to find the slightest difference in the distance. Should there be any the clock will not go, and as all the clocks are tested before being shipped, the defect is discovered and remedied. From the machine room the parts are taken to the

DIPPING ROOM

where they are immersed in a strong solution of acids, which relieves them of any particles of dust that may be sticking to them and gives them besides a polished appearance. In this room, too, the pendulums, dial rims and any other parts requiring it are nickel plated. The parts are taken from here into the movement room, where they are put together in remarkably quick time. In this room a young woman performs perhaps the most difficult and certainly the most tedious task in the factory. Her occupation is to pick up short pieces of fine wire with a pair of pincers and force them through the half dozen small holes which keep two of the tiny wheels on the pinion together. This seems to the reporter a much more difficult undertaking than threading a fine needle, yet the foreman said she could wire 2,500 of these daily, which would make 15,000 pieces of wire put through the holes with the pincers every day. In the pendulum and dial room the plates for the dials, which are made of metal, are pasted over with a white face on which are marked the hour hands (sic). The faces are merely printed sheets of paper cut to size, but dipped in a solution which permits of their being washed, and which prevents the color of the ink from spreading. When the different parts of the movements have been riveted together they are taken to the finishing room, where they are placed in the cases, the dials put on, the pendulums attached, the movements wound up, and the clocks set aside to see that they go smoothly and keep correct time before being shipped to fill orders. Now, although there are, properly speaking, but the plates, the ratchets and wheels, and the pinions comprising the works of a clock, there are innumerable little parts which all have to be handled and fitted in their places separately before either the ratchets and wheels or the pinions are completed, and these parts have consequently to be handled a great many times. The plates receive no less than 32 handlings before the movements are attached to them; the ratchets and wheels are handled 21 times, and the pinions and attachments no less than 264 times in an eight-day clock. Thus between 300 and 400 handlings of the various parts are necessary before a clock is completed. Yet some of these clocks are retailed for a dollar, which price could never have obtained had it not been for the invaluable aid of machinery.

THE CASE DEPARTMENT

Clock movements would look odd unless enclosed in cases, and this branch of the business is consequently a part and parcel of clock manufacture. Various kinds of wood are used for the cases, from pine to mahogany, and, in this department, too, so ably does the machinery do its work, that such things as planes and other tools for smoothing edges are unknown. In some of the more elaborate cases, however, carving has to be resorted to, but in ordinary cases the turning machines do the work. When the cases are glued and tacked together they are brought into the varnish room, where they are first stained and any openings in the wood filled in. They are afterwards varnished and made ready for the glass doors. Many of the doors are handsomely stained and ornamented from designs gotten up in the factory, some of them also being hand painted. A new feature in the striking apparatus of clocks has lately been introduced here, completely doing away with the sharp sound which causes nervous people to hold their fingers in their ears till the clock has got through telling the hour. This improvement consists in substituting for the bell which is struck by the striker, a coil of thin steel which when struck tolls out the hour as one would hear it from some far-off cathedral clock, and which produces an exceedingly pleasant sound. Two machinists are kept constantly employed in the factory making new parts for the machines which are constantly giving out owing to the high rate of speed at which it is absolutely necessary that they should be run. The day the reporter paid his visit to the factory was, perhaps, the happiest day in the week for the workmen, namely, pay day, and as the cashier dropped around with his basket of envelopes, thrusting one into each employee's hands, it fairly made the scribe's teeth water. To the foreman of the movement department, Mr. Thos. Foster, as well as to Mr. Jos. M. White, foreman of the case department, the thanks of the Tribune representative are specially due for courtesies extended, and the curious who visit the factory may rest assured these gentlemen will do all in their power to make the visit an agreeable and instructive one.

At the time of the reporter's visit to the factory, fifty employees worked there and all but two were natives of the area. The foreman of the movement department was Thomas W. Foster. According to the Hamilton city directories, Foster, clockmaker, lived in Hamilton from 1882 to 1885. The foreman of the case department was Joseph M. White. His name appears in the directory from 1877 as a carpenter. The name no longer appears in the directories after 1888.

Otherwise, very little information about the two clock companies in Hamilton was written. In the *Hamilton Spectator* of 3 March 1882, an article appeared about the new companies which had started recently in Hamilton and reference was made to the "new clock factory employing fifty hands." In the April 1882 issue, a statement appeared that "exports from Hamilton port included $175 of clocks to British Columbia." On 28 September 1882, the newspaper reported that "The Canada Clock Company of Hamilton exhibited fifty-five clocks in forty-three styles and also seven simple movements." This display was shown on the ground floor of the Palace at the Great Central Fair, Hamilton, Ontario. In 1884, the *Hamilton Spectator* stated that "The Canada Clock Company is expanding due to increased prosperity and new machinery has been added since 1882."

The Canada Clock Company is also mentioned in a book called *Hamilton and Its Industries*, by E.P. Morgan and F.L. Harvey, written in 1884. This book gives a description of goods available at the establishment of Levy Brothers and Scheuer, wholesale jewellers. Among other items, it describes clocks made in many countries and states that "The Canada Clock Company's goods make a fine show in this grand display of clocks valued at $10.00 per dozen to the huge regulators...."

Later in the life of the company, a slight change of name was used — "The Canada Clock Co'y Ltd."

Late in 1883, the company planned to diversify. In January 1884, a notice appeared in the *Canada Gazette* stating that the directors (Edmund Scheuer, Adam Rutherford, James Simpson, Charles Armstrong, Wm. Bell) of the Canada Clock Company (Limited) were expecting to apply for supplementary letters patent to enable them to carry on general manufacturing business in addition to manufacturing clocks.

They were prepared to do business by telephone. The name of the company was listed in the telephone directory of 1885. However, the Canada Clock Company was not destined to prosper. On 9 December 1884, the company declared bankruptcy. This fact was reported in a trade journal, *Canadian Jeweller*, then called *The Trader*, in January 1885.

On June 12, 1885, the *Ontario Gazette* carried the following notice:

NOTICE TO CREDITORS

Pursuant to a Winding up Order of the Chancery Division of the High Court of Justice dated 9th December, 1884 in the matter of the Canada Clock Company (Limited) and 45th Victoria Chapter 23, the creditors of the said Canada Clock Company are, on or before the 29th day of June, 1885 to send by post, prepaid to Adam Rutherford and Sherman E. Townsend, the liquidators of the said company, or either of them, their Christian and surnames, addresses and description of the full particulars of their claims, a statement of their accounts and the nature of their securities (if any) held by them, or in default thereof, they will be peremptorily excluded from the benefit of the said Winding up Order. Every Creditor holding any security is to produce the same before me at my chambers in Hamilton on the 30th day of June, 1885, at 10 o'clock, forenoon, being the time appointed for adjudication on the claims.

(signed)
M. O'Reilly
Master Supreme Court at Hamilton
Mackelcan, Gibson & Gausby
Solicitors for Liquidation

Although resistance was encountered in obtaining a complete list of the numerous creditors, it is known that three of the major creditors were: Schwob Brothers, Montreal, manufacturers and importers of diamonds and watches; J.E. Klotz of Preston, Ontario, manufacturer; and Plume Altwood & Co., of Boston, Massachusetts.

JUDICIAL SALE.

RE CANADA CLOCK COMPANY.

Tenders will be received by the liquidators hereinafter named, up to and including the 20th November, instant, for the purchase of that desirable factory property known as the Clock Factory at Hamilton, Ontario, together with the fixed and moveable machinery therein, including a 45 h. p. Wheelock Engine, manufactured by Goldie & McCulloch, and complete machinery, tools, dies, wood planers moulders, shapers, &c., for the manufacture of clocks, clock trimmings and cases. The factory is a large two storey-brick building, heated by steam lighted by gas, having a frontage of 120 feet on Kelly-street, and 64 feet on Cathcart-street, together with vacant ground 66 x 120.

The machinery is of the best kind and in first-rate order, and an excellent chance is afforded to manufacturers of clocks, furniture, musical instruments, &c., for a favourable investment.

An inventory of the fixed and moveable machinery, tools, &c., may be seen at any time at the office of the liquidators.

Tenders will be most favourably considered which offer the largest cash payments.

Further particulars and conditions will be made known on application to the liquidators, S. E. Townsend and Adam Rutherford, 6½ James-street South, or MacKelcan, Gibson, & Gausby, Liquidators' Solicitors, Hamilton.

Dated at Hamilton this 4th November, 1885.
(Signed) J. E. O'REILLY.
Master of Supreme Court at Hamilton.

Fig. 5 Judicial Sale — The Globe — 7 November 1885.

After the bankruptcy of the company, a number of references were made to it in newspapers, court proceedings and City Council meetings:

- In 1885, S.E. Townsend went to Montreal in an attempt to raise money to finance completion of partly manufactured clocks.
- In November 1885, the assets of the Canada Clock Company were offered for sale.
- In May 1886, parts of the clock and woodmaking machinery were offered for sale.
- On 23 May 1877, the factory, machinery and real estate were offered for sale for $15,000 and the offer was accepted.
- In January 1888, a court action was initiated by Sherman Edgar Townsend and John M. Gibson, plaintiffs against the Canada Clock Company, and James Simpson and Adam Rutherford, defendants.
- On 2 November 1888, court records indicate that Schwob proposed to buy the stock, estimated at $30,000, for 50¢ on the dollar.

The building that housed the clock factories was occupied in 1887-1888 by a manufacturer of lamps and bird cages. In 1889, and in the 1890s, it was used by E.T. Wright & Company, tinsmiths.

The building that originally housed the clock companies was demolished in 1971. An extra storey had been added, but the original window arrangement remained.

Fig. 6. The Old Factory Building in Hamilton shortly before demolition.
Courtesy of V. & S. Herzog.

PART II:
THE MEN INVOLVED IN THE COMPANIES

CHAPTER FOUR

The success or failure of any enterprise depends on a variety of factors, among which the most important are the skills of management, the quality of the product or service and, invariably, just pure luck. The history of the three clock companies operating in Whitby and Hamilton between 1872 and 1885 demonstrated that one favourable circumstance was the quality of their product. This factor alone, however, was not sufficient to make the companies successful. With regard to the management, it is evident that they were men of speculation rather than skillful managers of the clock trade. The only person associated with the companies who apparently knew anything about the clockmaking business was John F. Collins, a machinist and jeweller by trade. However, John's brothers, William F. and Edward S., were involved with the Canada Clock Company, Whitby, from its inception. Therefore, it was considered appropriate by the authors to describe in detail the life, work and family of the three Collins brothers and to continue with the other persons associated with the clock companies mentioned previously in the book.

WILLIAM FITZPATRICK COLLINS

William Fitzpatrick Collins (b. 1846, d. 3 November 1895) was the eldest son of Robert H. Collins (b. 1809, d. 27 November 1887), a Quaker by religion and a veterinary surgeon by profession, and Sarah Fitzpatrick (b. 1826, d. 4 February 1902). Both parents were born in Dublin, Ireland, and immigrated to Canada West with their two sons in 1848-1849, settling in Whitby Township. Here Edward was born in 1849 and John F. was born in 1852. By 1855, the family was living in Guelph, Ontario. The family moved again in the mid-1870s to Hamilton, but records exist indicating that Dr. Collins was there in 1865.

William F., John F., and Edward were in Whitby early in 1872 intending to manufacture clocks. In March 1872, William and his brothers were granted permission by the Town Council to erect a steam engine of ten horsepower for manufacturing purposes. From June to December of that year, the brothers assembled and, in some cases, made machinery for their endeavour. Clocks were made in January 1873.

In August 1873, William decided that it would be to their advantage to incorporate, and with a group of men from Port Hope, he gave notice of his intention in the *Canada Gazette*. (See Appendix 3) However, J.H. Greenwood took over the company in the autumn of 1873. William went to live with his parents in Hamilton and worked there as a clerk.

Around 1882 his father retired and William moved with the family to Toronto to work as a clerk and commercial traveller. After the death of his father in 1887, William moved in 1888 to Brookfield, New Jersey, where he was a merchant. He died in New Jersey in 1895 and is buried in the family plot in Mount Pleasant Cemetery, Toronto.

William's mother, Sarah, lived in Toronto until 1901 when she moved to Chicago. She died in Chicago in 1902 and is also buried in Mount Pleasant Cemetery. Records show that Heloize Collins, a child of four who died in 1890, is also buried in the plot.

JOHN F. COLLINS

John F. Collins (b. 1852, d. after 1920) was the fourth son of Robert H. Collins and Sarah. John was born in Whitby, Ontario, moving with the family to Guelph by 1855. According to the 1871 census, John was a machinist, implying that he apprenticed or studied his trade in an established institution. It is not known where John F. Collins took his training, but in 1872 he joined his brother William in Whitby to set up a factory to manufacture clocks. When J.H. Greenwood became president of the Whitby clock company in the autumn of 1873, John became manager of the company. Unfortunately, the clock company under Greenwood was not successful, and by April 1875, the company was taken over by Colonel James Wallace. Col. Wallace decided to find out if the company could be run profitably and, when he discovered that this was impossible, there was little work for Collins to do.

In early May 1876, he was invited to join the newly formed Hamilton Clock Company in Hamilton. He moved to that city and lived with his parents and brother Edward at 36 Bay Street. John was appointed mechanical superintendent while James Simpson was president and George Lee was business manager.

A dispute arose between Collins and the other two men. A court case resulted and the court ruled in favour of the defendants, Simpson and Lee. Collins broke his association with these men in 1879.

In February 1881, the company changed ownership and at the same time the name of the company changed from Hamilton Clock Company to Canada Clock Company (Limited), Hamilton. John F. Collins was not a shareholder in the new company and was not involved in it in any way. In the census of 1881, John was listed as a jeweller.

The Collins family moved to Toronto in 1883, and John followed them in 1884. He lived with his family until around 1893. During the period that he lived in Toronto, he was a traveller for the Pure Gold Manufacturing Company. The company was based in Fairport, New York, and had a plant in Toronto at 11 Colborne Avenue. It manufactured baking powder, sold pure spices and carried other similar products. Collins later became manager of another firm, The Gold Seal Manufacturing Co.

Fig. 7 Advertisement for Pure Gold Manufacturing Co. 1885 Toronto Directory.

Fig. 8 "Pure Gold" Container The Griffith Collection.

In the mid-1890s, John F. Collins moved to Chicago, where he lived at least until 1920.

Although it has been reported that John F. Collins was a lumber dealer as well as the man associated with the first Canada Clock Company and the Hamilton Clock Company, further research by the authors has established the facts otherwise. John Collins, the lumberman, did not use a middle initial. Furthermore, he is listed in Hamilton directories during the years when it is known that John F. Collins was living in Guelph and Whitby. Finally, John Collins, the lumberman, was considerably older than John F. Collins. In fact he was older than John F. Collins' mother.

EDWARD SKELTON COLLINS

Associated with John F. in the clock manufacturing enterprise was an older brother, Edward Skelton Collins (b. 1849, d. 3 February 1920). Edward, who was born in Whitby, moved to Guelph with his parents, and in 1866 took part as a private in the Fenian Raid in Toronto and Goderich. He was awarded a service medal on 9 February 1900. In 1872 he returned to Whitby to work with John at the Canada Clock Company. In late 1875 or early 1876, he went to Hamilton and lived with his parents. When John came to Hamilton to work for the Hamilton Clock Company, Edward joined him working as a clock finisher for a few years. Edward was a sign painter by profession and after leaving the clock factory pursued his profession and established his own business and had various partners. Edward married Maria Frances Van Brocklin (b. 1868, d. 1955) in the early 1890s, but had no children. He and his wife are buried in Hamilton Cemetery. (For further family see chapter 11.)

JOHN HAMER GREENWOOD

John Hamer Greenwood (b. 20 January 1829, d. 15 July 1902) was associated with the Canada Clock Company, Whitby, from 1873 to early March 1875. He was born in Radnorshire, Wales, and came to Canada in 1849 or 1850, settling in Hamer's Corners, Canada West, a place named after his uncle, John Hamer. Hamer's Corners was located about a mile from the present centre of the City of Whitby.

Upon his arrival, Greenwood having no money and very little education, started to work as a labourer for James Wallace, a contractor building the court house for the proposed Town of Whitby. His first job as a labourer with Wallace was mixing mortar and carrying hod.

Being ambitious, he obtained enough education to enter the Whitby Model School and was one of its first graduates. Upon graduation, he became a teacher at the "Common" School in Whitby for a short time. By 1857-58 he was a law student and, in order to make money, he offered loans at "reasonable terms." At the same time he was buying and selling real estate. When he graduated, he opened up an office on Brock Street, Whitby. In various advertisements he offered his services as barrister, solicitor in chancery, notary public and attorney-at-law. Greenwood was a "man in a hurry," getting involved in almost anything he could put his hands on. For example, in 1858 he was secretary of the School Board, member of the Whitby Literacy and Scientific Society, secretary of the Masonic Composite Lodge and debator in the Whitby Debating Society. He took the negative side in the debate "Resolved that a Federal Union of BNA Provinces Would Add To Their Prosperity." In 1859, in addition to all his 1858 activities, he became second vice-president of the Whitby Mechanics Institute, rising to first vice-president the year after. Records also show that during this period he owned a farm called "Mitchell Farm" west of Whitby, where he built a very large residence.

In addition to his law career, J. Hamer served on committees of local government and in 1872 was elected as mayor of Whitby and served in this capacity until 1875. He served again as mayor in 1883.

In the early autumn of 1873, J. Hamer added to his businesses the Canada Clock Company, Whitby. This company specialized in the manufacture of ogee weight clocks and had been in

Fig. 9 A Monument Marks Their Grave.

Fig. 10 Commemorative Stained Glass Window.

production since January 1873. In this factory John F. Collins was the manager and Greenwood was appointed president. The company was only fairly successful. Unfortunately, Greenwood ran into financial difficulties, and he declared bankruptcy in March 1875. His financial difficulties were caused by his assuming too many responsibilities at one time, thus spreading his attention too thinly in his many business and civic duties. In fact, J. Hamer had run into financial difficulties before. A previous venture into the manufacture of sewing machines resulted in a failure. A meeting of all his creditors was held at the factory on 9 March 1875, under the chairmanship of Mr. Coulthard. An article in the 11 March 1875 issue of the *Whitby Chronicle* gave details of the assets and liabilities of Greenwood. It also included a statement concerning the future of the clock factory as recorded at the creditors' meeting. According to the article, the factory was worth $46,000 and the intention of the creditors was to have the clock business continue "with the view of working up all the material and completing the unfinished work now on hand. This is decidedly at once the best and most economical course and will likely eventually lead to the formation of a strong joint Stock Company for carrying on the business." The company passed into the hands of James Wallace in April 1875.

After his death, the *Oshawa Vindicator* of 18 July 1902 reported that Mr. John Hamer Greenwood "was several times crushed beneath the wheel of fortune, but always managed to come out again in a short time. He was noted as a financier who could always wiggle out of a hole, but his enterprising and speculative nature pulled him back into the hole as fast as he could struggle his way out."

Another document obtained from the Whitby Public Library states that "according to information obtained from older residents of the town, it appears that J.H. Greenwood was something of a notorious character, a heavy drinker and known for his shrewd and sometimes questionable legal deals."

On 14 September 1865, J. Hamer married Charlotte (b. 19 May 1846, d. 24 July 1902), daughter of Thomas Churchill Hubbard of United Loyalist stock. Charlotte was born in Brougham, Ontario. The family belonged to the Church of England. (For family see chapter 11)

J.H. Greenwood chose the spelling of his middle name to be "Hamer." (J. Hamer's son chose the spelling "Hamar," following the spelling used by his grandmother and family in Britain.) Apparently J. Hamer chose this spelling in honour of his uncle, after whom Hamer's Corners was named. John Hamer was afflicted with severe deafness during the latter part of his life. He died at the age of 73, on 15 July 1902, after having been stricken by paralysis. His wife died nine days later. Both were buried in the Union Cemetery, Oshawa, Ontario.

The children of J. Hamer and Charlotte erected a monument in their memory. On one face it reads: "In loving memory of our Father, John Hamer Greenwood, Barrister-in-Law, Born at Llanbister, Radnorshire, Wales, Jan. 20, 1829, died at Whitby, Ont. July 15, 1902. Fifty years of a strenuous life and every minute a fight." On the other face it reads: "In loving memory of our Mother, Charlotte, wife of John Hamer Greenwood. Born at Brougham, Ont. May 19th, 1846, died at Whitby, Ont. July 24, 1902. And her children shall rise up and call her blessed."

A stained glass window in All Saints Anglican Church, Whitby, was dedicated by their children to the memory of John Hamer Greenwood and his wife, Charlotte.

JAMES WALLACE

James Wallace (b. 3 March 1814, d. 10 July 1882) was born in Kincardineshire, Scotland, and settled in the Whitby area of Upper Canada before 1840. James married Elspeth Dow (b. November 1814, d. 13 December 1913) on 9 July 1840 at her family residence in Whitby Township. The marriage was performed by Rev. James George. Elspeth was the third daughter of William Dow, originally from Banffshire, Scotland, who settled in the Eastern Townships before coming to the Whitby area and purchasing the Glen Dhu farm on the third Concession of Whitby Township. He had entered "Canada" in 1833 when he drove a team of horses across the ice at Ogdensburg.

By the time of his marriage, James Wallace was well established in Whitby Township. He was a graduate of Whitby "Model School" and had been a teacher for a short time. In 1840 he was a merchant and by 1851 was proprietor of a large general store at Hamer's Corners, now part of Whitby. He also owned property in the 1840s on Concession 6, Lot 21.

James Wallace was not content to settle down with one business. Over the next 35 years James Wallace's name would be associated with many business ventures, one of which, in the 1870s, was the Canada Clock Company, Whitby.

In 1851, James Wallace was engaged in the wheat and flour business, but realized the need for a railway. In 1852, he and eight other leading businessmen of Whitby held a successful public meeting to promote the building of a railway. As a result of the meeting, "the Port Whitby and Lake Huron Railroad Co." was incorporated in April 1853. Unfortunately, little was accomplished in the way of making the dream a reality. The *Whitby Chronicle* of 1859 was still discussing the likelihood of the success of such an undertaking.

In the meantime, James Wallace was proving himself to be a most successful business contractor. His bid was successful as contractor for building the county buildings in Whitby, which was to be the "County Town." His name as contractor appears on the cornerstone, laid with great pomp and ceremony on 30 June 1853. This building, the Whitby Centennial Building, remains today.

Other buildings contracted by Wallace are mentioned in the *Whitby Free Press* of 9 August 1978. A large two-storey building on the west side of Brock Street, north of Colborne, was built in 1859 and stood 42 years until destroyed by fire in 1901. A large brick mansion, later known as Burr Lodge, on Centre Street South at Keith Street, still stands today. This building, now divided into apartments, was at one time the home of James Wallace. A number of brick cottages and two sets of row housing, built by Wallace, were used as military barracks. One set of the two-storey buildings was later known as Vanstone Terrace.

Another project completely financed by Wallace was barracks and officers quarters for the militia. These buildings stand today at Centre Street near Burr Lodge. The house on the corner of Keith Street and Centre Street is thought to be the officers' quarters and to the south of it, the commanding officer's home.

In addition to his construction work, other occupations attracted James Wallace. This is evidenced by the varied advertisements which appeared in the newspapers. In February 1853, the *Ontario Reporter*, a newspaper in Whitby, carried several advertisements in which Wallace announced that he was agent for Fire, Life and General Insurance and represented several companies. He held this position for at least two years.

By December 1856, Wallace had purchased exclusive rights to the manufacture of "Headley's Marbleized Granite, a cheap, beautiful and durable building material." He hoped to begin manufacture "on a large scale" the following spring.

It was also during this period in the 1850s that Wallace played an active role in local politics. He served on the town council from 1855, when the Town of Whitby was incorporated, until 1857. In 1856, Wallace was mayor of Whitby. During his mayorality, an issue came up concerning debentures for which he was to be severely criticized.

In 1856, debentures were printed for the town, each of which represented 83 pounds, six shillings and eight pence, and these were placed on sale. In due course, Wallace was accused of "losing" four of these debentures. Notices were put in the newspapers cautioning the public against purchasing the debentures. After much accusation and publicity, a special committee was appointed by the town council to investigate the issue. Upon investigation, Wallace was exonerated. The committee announced that no debentures were lost because the ones in question were merely blanks, never filled in, signed or completed. New debentures were printed and issued.

In response, Wallace wrote to the council complaining of the stigma cast upon his character during the search for the "missing" debentures. In 1859, Mr. Higgens of the *Chronicle* reported "For our part — whatever Mr. Wallace may think to the contrary — there is no one who would be farther from spreading a report injurious to Mr. Wallace's character than the editor of the *Chronicle*."

Fig. 11 Col. James Wallace
Courtesy Whitby Historical Society.

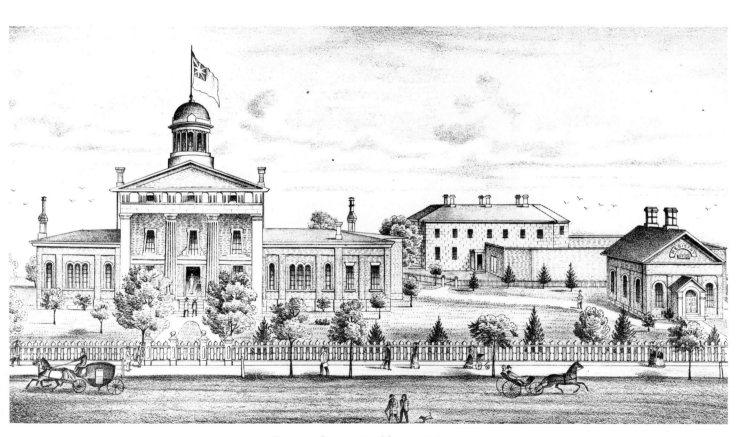

Fig. 12 County Buildings, Whitby
From the Illustrated Historical Atlas of the County of Ontario, Ontario, 1877.

This statement of Mr. Higgens' is rather hard to believe completely because, at the time it was made, Wallace was editor and publisher of a rival newspaper to the *Whitby Chronicle* called *The Whitby Watchman.*

Fig. 13 The Whitby Watchman, Thursday, August 25, 1859.

Wallace published this newspaper from 1857 to 1861. Although certainly not considered so by Wallace, the newspaper was labeled as highly controversial. The two editors attacked one another in print. On one occasion in 1861, Higgens reported in the *Chronicle* about "a murderous assault on his person by Mr. Wallace." Higgens claimed that he was "knocked down senseless from behind with a club by that most notorious of outrageous scoundrels, James Wallace." This action resulted in the arrest of Wallace. Court records do not indicate that a conviction in this regard followed. Wallace, however, was charged with perjury in 1861.

Another business venture undertaken by James Wallace in 1858 was the acquisition of the Whitby Soap and Candle factory, also known as the Glasgow Soap Works. He advertised for "butchers' and other tallow and lard" and offered hand soap "of a quality equal, if not superior, to the best Toronto-made."

Other businesses he was associated with at one time or another include a brick plant on the old Gilmour property and a sash and door factory.

In July 1869, Wallace went to Red River to work with the Red River surveying party. He returned in September, enthusiastic about the potential in the area for farming because of the richness of the loam. He was looking forward to returning later in the year. The *Whitby Chronicle* carried articles recounting his adventures in the west.

James Wallace was not involved with the Canada Clock Company, Whitby, at its inception in 1872. Although John F. Collins' name appears on nearly every clock paper as manager of the clock factory, no clock paper has been seen by the authors exhibiting both the Wallace and Greenwood names.

Another reason to believe that Wallace was not associated with the clock company in the beginning was that during the early period of the company Wallace was not in the country. In January 1873 Wallace was posted to Britain as a Canadian Immigration Agent. A large complimentary supper with Mayor Greenwood and some 40 men in attendance was given for the "guest of honour, Mr. Wallace, with speech and song, a happy evening quickly passed away." Wallace returned after eight months to Whitby and was reappointed. Thus, he was away for a considerable period of time in 1874. In February 1875, Wallace took up duties in Whitby as an assessor and the *Chronicle* reported that he would "bring intimate knowledge of the value of property and honesty" to the position.

In April 1875, Wallace purchased the Canada Clock Company from Greenwood's assignee and proceeded to test the profitability of the company. Despite his efforts he soon decided that the factory was losing money. Movements were imported from the Ansonia Clock Company, Connecticut, U.S.A., to complete empty clock cases, remaining afer movement-making ceased at Whitby. This occurred either as a result of the decision by Wallace that the factory was not profitable, or after the fire in the factory on 3 December 1875. However, the fire brought down the final curtain. The insurance covered only one quarter of the loss. Two auction sales of clocks and factory items were held, one in June 1876 and the second in May 1877, in order to help recoup his losses.

By 1880, Wallace moved to Oak Park, near Chicago, where he found ready employment due to his connection with railway matters. He thus recovered some of his wealth in the United States.

While not always successful in his business ventures, records prove that few could match his devotion to military matters. Although his military career was not without difficult times, his contributions were many. He was recorded as an ensign in the local militia as early as 1846. He was responsible for forming a large volunteer militia company in Whitby long before there were such companies in other communities in the area. During the Crimean War, in 1854, many militia companies were unified for the purpose of national defense, and on 31 March 1856, Wallace founded the Whitby Volunteer Highland Rifle Company, of which he was the captain and later lieutenant colonel. He personally supplied uniforms and equipment for more than 40 men and built the barracks for them. By 1858, the Highland Rifle Company of Whitby was the sixth company in position of seniority.

In September 1859, the *Whitby Chronicle* carried the following report: "Our town was very much enlivened on evenings of late by drilling, marching and military evolutions of Captain Wallace's Highland Rifle Company. About forty active young men of the town have now joined and have arrived at a high degree of military training under the capable discipline of Sergeant Robinson. The officers and men have very creditable military bearing considering the short time since the formation of the company. They go to Toronto fully equipped and accoutered to the provincial show this year, and we venture to say they will bear favourable comparison with any military company on the ground."

In 1860, the Whitby Volunteer Highland Rifle Company became the Number 6 Company of the Second Battalion Volunteer Militia Rifles of Canada which, two years later, became the Queen's Own Rifles of Canada. In September 1860, the rifle company formed a guard of honour for the visit of the Prince of Wales to Whitby. With Captain Wallace in command, they escorted the prince's carriage from the Grand Trunk Railway Station to a waiting boat in the harbour. Wallace's son William, 12 years of age, was an onlooker.

On 24 May 1861, the battalion paraded at the Parliament buildings in honour of the Queen's birthday. In June 1861, however, it was reported in the *Whitby Chronicle* by rival Mr. Higgens that, due to the "infamous conduct of James Wallace, he would be deprived of commission as Captain of the Highland Rifle Company." The same paper contained the report of his alleged "murderous assault" on Higgens. It was apparent that Wallace's rank was retained because, in March 1866, Captain Wallace commanded a composite company of militia during the Fenian Raid scare. His men were posted at Port Colborne. In June, he and his men took part in the Battle of Ridgeway.

By September 1866, the 34th Ontario Battalion of Infantry (now the Ontario Regiment) was formed with Lieutenant Colonel Silas B. Fairbanks of Oshawa as commanding officer and Wallace, now a major, as second in command.

He was a major when he accompanied the Red River expedition in 1869. He then rose to the rank of lieutenant colonel and commanded the 34th Regiment from April 1872 to January 1874. During this time he was away from Canada for two periods of eight months when he served as "Dominion Immigration Agent to England." In January 1874, it was reported in the *Official Gazette* that he had been superceded and deprived of his rank because he had been absent without leave. This order was considered unfair by the *Whitby Chronicle* because he was away on government business. Also, he was a favourite among the militia as "he stood up for the rights and privileges of both officers and men." He had donated both time and money to the cause. It did not take long for the misunderstanding to be cleared up, and Lieutenant Colonel Wallace commanded the regiment from August 1874 to March 1880.

In addition to his business and military activities, Wallace was a prominent Mason and was a charter member of the Composite Lodge in Whitby in 1852 and Master of the Lodge in 1858. He was a charter member and trustee of the Free Church (Presbyterian) of Whitby.

Wallace suffered a heart attack on 10 July 1882 at his home in Oak Park, Illinois. He was

68 years old. The doctor diagnosed the immediate cause of death as angina. He was interred at Forest Home Cemetery, Forest Park, Illinois, on 16 July 1882. He was later moved to Rosehill Cemetery in Chicago, but there is no further record of where the body lies. Other members of his family are buried at Rosehill Cemetery. These include his wife, Elspeth, who lived 34 years in Chicago after the death of her husband and son James Jr. (For family see chapter 11)

GEORGE LEE

The Hamilton Clock Company was established in Hamilton in 1876. George Lee was its business manager and his name appears on the labels of the clocks along with the names of James Simpson and John F. Collins. In some instances, George's name appears alone on the label.

George Lee (b. 1830, d. 17 April 1891) was born at Bally Bay, Inneskillen, Ireland. He came to America around 1850, settling at St. Louis, Missouri. A brother, Robert, and his wife, Annie, lived in Memphis, Tennessee. During the Civil War, George came north and located in Hamilton where he commenced business as a wholesale and retail fruit dealer on King Street W. George branched out to deal, by 1865, in "fruit, oysters and game." He sold his wholesale business in 1874 and, with his son William George, opened a restaurant and entered the restaurant and hotel business at 66-68 King Street W., Hamilton.

In 1875, George acquired an interest in the Gardiner Sewing Machine Company, which he subsequently sold in 1879 to Mr. F.M. Willson.

By 1881, George and William George were in failing health, and by 1885 had sold the hotel and restaurant business. They went south for a year, but did not regain their health. After a long illness, George died in April 1891. The funeral was a Masonic funeral at which Adam Rutherford, then Worshipful Master of the Lodge, took part.

In addition to being an active Mason during his lifetime and a member of St. John Lodge, George Lee had other interests. In 1870, he was president of the Horticultural Society. He was interested in civic politics and represented Ward 5 on city council in 1875 and again in 1877. He was a "staunch Conservative" and took a great interest in all levels of politics. He was a member of the Irish Protestant Benevolent Society.

George Lee's wife, Ellen Colvin, died about 1896. Their only son, William, was born in 1859. William George, however, was not well. He suffered from a painful illness of the spinal cord which incapacitated him for 12 years prior to his death on May 24, 1897, at the age of 38. He did not marry.

The will of William George Lee, a very detailed document, divided a substantial estate among cousins, friends, servants and charities. Provision was made for the establishment of the W.G. Lee Ward for incurables, unable to pay, at St. Peter's Infirmary.

JAMES SIMPSON

James Simpson (b. 1832, d. 13 August 1907) was associated with both clock companies in Hamilton. He was born in Scotland and he and his family were Presbyterian by faith. James came to Hamilton around 1853 and opened two grocery stores, one on south John Street and another on Market Square. In the 1860s, James formed a partnership with James M. Stuart, creating a company called Simpson, Stuart and Company. This enterprise was one of the first and best-known wholesale grocery businesses in Canada and conducted business all over the Dominion. The company was based at 61 McNab Street, Hamilton. Mr. Stuart was manager of the company.

In the summer of 1876, James Simpson became involved with the Hamilton Clock Company in the capacity of president. His name appears in this capacity on most of the Hamilton Clock Company labels.

When the Canada Clock Company Ltd. was incorporated in 1881, Simpson was made president and held 100 shares. He was trustee of the company as well as a provisional director. During this time he was also associated with his own company, Simpson, Stuart and Company.

Fig 14. *James Simpson*
from the Hamilton Herald, 14 August 1907.

Fig. 15
Headstone of James Simpson.

In 1885, he formed a company with his son James Jr., called James Simpson and Son. They were "grocery brokers and commission merchants." Also, at some time during his business career, Simpson was president of the Dominion Insurance Company. He retired from all business activitiy in 1902.

According to the *Hamilton Spectator*, Mr. Simpson, in his younger days, was an enthusiastic curler. "He skipped the rink that brought the world's championship to Hamilton." When no longer able to curl, he continued to be an interested spectator.

Simpson was married twice. His first wife died around 1854, leaving a son, William Simpson. William went, as a young man, to live in Winnipeg, Manitoba.

Around 1855, James Simpson married Marion Cowie Hood (1828-1901) (for descendants see chapter 11), who had been married previously and had two sons, Thomas Hood and John Hood. Son Thomas lived in Hamilton. John Hood was proprietor of a hotel in Buffalo in 1901 and in New York in 1907.

James Simpson died on 13 August 1907 and is buried with other members of his family in Hamilton Cemetery.

Fig. 16 Adam Rutherford.

ADAM RUTHERFORD

Adam Rutherford (b. 1842, d. 29 June 1917) became manager of the newly formed Canada Clock Company in Hamilton in 1881. He remained associated with the company until its liquidation in December 1884.

According to his death certificate, he was born in Caledon Township, Canada West. His father was Alexander Rutherford, a Scotsman, and his mother's name was given simply as Miss McLean. The family belonged to the Church of England.

Adam married Sarah Lester (b. 18 August 1846, d. 8 January 1890), daughter of Thomas Lester and Margaret Mussen, on 26 October 1870. Adam taught school in Caledon Township before moving to Hamilton, where he worked for the waterworks department, first as a clerk and later as a bookkeeper.

By 1875, Adam had become an insurance agent and held the position of insurance inspector for the Victoria Mutual Fire Insurance Company. After being a member of the city council for the year 1880, Adam formed a partnership with his brother-in-law, Col. Thomas W. Lester. The firm also dealt in real estate and occasionally advertised as being auctioneers. This partnership continued until about 1904.

In addition to his insurance business, Adam was manager of the Canada Clock Company Ltd., the successor of the Hamilton Clock Company. Rutherford owned 60 shares of the clock company's stock and was one of the company's trustees. When the company went into liquidation, Adam Rutherford and Sherman E. Townsend were named as liquidators to whom creditors were to state their claims. As a result, Adam was involved in a court action concerning the Canada Clock Company in 1888.

In 1894, Adam became interested in another venture, the Hamilton, Grimsby and Beamsville Electric Railway. He became secretary-treasurer of the enterprise.

After the death of his first wife in 1890, Adam married Maria Nelles (b. 1856, d. 1938) in the mid-1890s. (For descendants see chapter 11)

By 1904, Adam was no longer partner with Lester. He formed another company with George H. Rilett as partner. This company of Rutherford and Rilett were also auctioneers, real estate and insurance agents. This partnership continued until 1907 when Adam left Hamilton to live in Grimsby, the home of his wife's family, and he continued to work for the Hamilton, Grimsby and Beamsville Electric Railway.

Throughout his adult life, Adam was an active Mason. In 1891, as Worshipful Master of the Masonic Lodge, he conducted the funeral service of his Masonic brother, George Lee, who had been associated with the clock companies.

Adam Rutherford died in Grimsby, Ontario, and is buried in the City of Hamilton Cemetery.

JOHN M. LESTER

John M. Lester (b. 30 January 1849, d. 6 October 1906) was secretary-treasurer of the Canada Clock Company Ltd. during the years 1882-1885. He did not hold any company stock.

John was a descendant of James Mussen (d. 1740), a Huguenot who settled in Ireland. The grandfather of John M. Lester, John Mussen (b. 1773, d. 1825) married Jane Martin on 21 July 1819 and had three children. John's mother, Margaret (b. 23 March 1821, d. 25 November 1910), was the only child who survived to adulthood, and with her mother, Jane, she immigrated to Canada in 1828 and settled in Toronto.

John M. Lester's father, Thomas Lester (b. 8 March 1814, d. 23 March 1888), also emigrated with his family from Ireland around 1830 and settled in Upper Canada.

Thomas Lester married his first cousin, Margaret Mussen, and moved to the States. (A complete family tree is available from J. Varkaris.)

Each of the three children of Margaret and Thomas Lester was directly or indirectly associated with the Canada Clock Company Ltd., Hamilton, Ontario. Sarah (b. 18 August 1846, d. 8 January 1890) married Adam Rutherford, manager of the Canada Clock Company Ltd. Colonel Thomas William Lester (b. 14 April 1854, d. 17 October 1932) was a partner of Adam Rutherford in his insurance and real estate business for many years, and John M. was secretary-treasurer of the clock company while his brother-in-law held the position of manager.

John M. was born in Halimand County, Indiana, U.S.A. He went to the University of Edinburgh, Scotland, where he graduated as a medical doctor and returned to the United States to practice. He practiced medicine, however, for a very short time. According to his grandniece, the reason for his leaving medicine was that "he was so tender hearted he could not stand to see the suffering." He then set up a very successful druggist business.

On 11 June 1878, he married Blanche Graham (b. 1854, d. January 1901), who had been born in Lackawax (sic), Pennsylvania, the daughter of Martin D. Graham, Port Jervis, New York. Blanche, according to her obituary, was a painter and "a most estimable lady." A number of her paintings are treasured by the family. Shortly after they were married, John M. and his wife moved to Hamilton, Ontario, and by 1882 he was working for the Canada Clock Company Ltd. After the liquidation of the company, John joined his brother-in-law's firm at 17-19 King Street West, Hamilton.

After the death of his wife in 1901, John lived with his sister Sarah Rutherford and her family.

John died on 6 October 1906 following an operation made necessary by a sudden illness. John had one son, John M., who died as an infant. John, his wife and son are buried in Hamilton Cemetery.

EDMUND SCHEUER

Edmund Scheuer (b. 30 October 1847, d. 2 July 1943) was both a director and a shareholder of the Canada Clock Company Ltd., Hamilton. During the period of his association with the clock company, Scheuer was a partner in the Levy Brothers and Company, wholesale and retail jewellers.

Edmund, son of Isaac and Yohanna Scheuer, was born in Berncasel, Prussia. After attending school in Lorraine, in 1865 he decided to work in Paris, France, instead of returning to his homeland where Jews were being persecuted. He came to Hamilton, Ontario, in 1871 and worked for Levy Brothers.

Edmund Scheuer was very active in the Jewish community. In 1872, he organized the first Jewish Sabbath School in the province, and on 2 July 1873 he married Ada Strauss. By 1882 he had established the first Jewish Reformed Synagogue in Canada.

In 1886, he moved to Toronto and opened a wholesale jewellery firm. He joined Toronto's Board of Trade and remained a member for over 50 years. In addition, he was a member of the Holy Blossom Synagogue for over 51 years and held every official position possible. He founded the first Jewish Benevolent Society in 1892 and was active in the Canada Club, the Empire Club and belonged to other associations. In 1902, he was appointed Justice of the Peace. In 1927, Scheuer House was named in his honour.

Scheuer had a great ability in assessing human qualities. Two incidents worth noting in this regard are recounted in the book *The Pequegnat Story, the Family and the Clocks*, by Jane and Costas Varkaris, and are quoted below:

> When a farmer wanted a particular watch that Arthur (Pequegnat) did not have in stock in his shop (Mildmay), he walked ninety miles to Hamilton to look for one. On this trip to Hamilton, Arthur not only found the watch that he wanted, but also met a man by the name of Edmund Scheuer, who helped him.... Having found the watch, Arthur suggested that he would return for it when the farmer gave him the money. Scheuer, however, insisted that he take the watch with him and pay for it when the farmer paid him.... (Several years later) Arthur was in the shop in Berlin and Ed Scheuer dropped in to see him. Ed thought that he looked down in the mouth. Arthur confessed that he was a bit worried, as he had to meet a bill of $500.00 and didn't have the money. Nothing more was said and Arthur went home to dinner. When he went back to the shop, a young fellow came in with a package wrapped in brown paper. Arthur opened it and there was the amount of $500.00 without a note or word of explanation. It was gratefully accepted and quickly paid back. Arthur was appreciative of Scheuer's kindness and named his oldest son, Edmond.

It should be noted that Arthur Pequegnat went on to bigger things by establishing the only successful Canadian clock company many years later.

Edmund Scheuer was the only man who was on close terms with principals of three of Canada's clock companies. He saw in his lifetime the beginning and the end of the Hamilton Clock Company, the second Canada Clock Company and the Arthur Pequegnat Clock Company.

In 1943, he died in Toronto, where he is buried in Holy Blossom Cemetery.

WILLIAM D. LONG

William D. Long (b. 18 November 1840, d. 13 February 1920) held 40 shares in the Canada Clock Company Ltd., Hamilton, in 1881. He was the eldest son of P.G. and Isabella M. Long of

Farmington, Missouri. After his schooling, he worked in the United States as a farmer, a tanner and a steamboat operator. In 1862, he left United States for Canada, where he was engaged in the wool business. He, with his partner and brother-in-law, George H. Bisby (d. 1912), succeeded A.S. Woodruff and Company, the first wool house in Canada, and later moved to McNab Street, to the site of the old barracks, where they remained for 25 years. Their next move was to the corner of John and Main streets. According to a book titled *Hamilton and Its Industries*, by the mid-1880s, the firm handled approximately three million pounds of wool, including Canadian short wool and large quantities of imported wool for Canadian manufacturers. The firm had a reputation which "stands the highest wherever wool is marketable throughout the length and breadth of our fair land.... Men ship their wool to this firm from Nova Scotia, New Brunswick, Manitoba and British Columbia, with the utmost confidence, and just as safe as the bank, always receive the highest market price, as promptly as a clock ticks without barter or abatement." According to the obituary in the newspaper after Long's death, the firm of Long and Bisby was founded on mutual trust. Neither partner recorded how much each took out of the firm for his own needs.

In addition to his wool business and his interest in the clock company, William Long was vice-president of the National Life Insurance Company of Toronto and vice-president of the Imperial Cotton Company.

Long and Bisby donated the land for the building of the Mountain Sanitarium in Hamilton and continued to support it generously. Later, Long donated $75,000 for building a nurses' home at the sanitarium.

William D. Long never married. He lived with his sister, Jane, the wife of his partner, G.H. Bisby. Another sister, Mrs. T.S. Wilson, lived in Missouri. A brother, John Hugh Long, lived in Hamilton.

W. Long died of pneumonia on 13 February 1920.

JOHN HARVEY

John Harvey (b. circa 1834, d. 17 February 1915) was a shareholder in the Canada Clock Company Ltd., Hamilton. He was born in Scotland and came to Canada as a young man. For many years he headed the wholesale wool firm of John Harvey & Company, commission merchants and wool brokers. The company was one of the largest exporting concerns in Canada during the last quarter of the nineteenth century. In the twentieth century, he carried on a successful insurance business and was an agent for Sun Life Insurance.

As a young man, he was an avid bowler and curler and was a member of the Thistle Curling Club's Tankard Rink. He skipped Tankard Rinks in many victories. It is reasonable to believe that his interest in the Canada Clock Company might have been sparked by his acquaintance with another curler well known in Hamilton, James Simpson, the president of the Canada Clock Company Ltd.

John Harvey had three sons and three daughters. In 1915, at the time of his death, Stuart lived in Manila, Philippine Islands. James was in the armed forces and George R. lived in Hamilton. Harvey was survived by three daughters, Mrs. Helen Edmundson (d. 3 October 1947) wife of Thomas L. Edmundson of San Diego, California; Mrs. Laura Sey (d. 19 January 1963); and Miss Florence Harvey of Hamilton (d. 12 July 1968).

At his death, his obituary stated that John Harvey was "a man of highest honour and integrity and was held in highest esteem."

PART III: THE CLOCKS

CHAPTER FIVE
ARE THEY TRULY CANADIAN?

A study of movements used by the three Canadian companies (hereafter called Canada Clock Company I, Hamilton Clock Company and Canada Clock Company II) may well begin with an elementary question: Did they make their own? One of the major objectives of this chapter is to provide some answers. In the past, some observers and collectors of Canadian clocks have been quick to label the three companies as mere importers and assemblers of American parts and cases. Others have found this assumption unacceptable. There have been too many clues that did not lead to such a simple conclusion. It is only fair to state at the outset that the authors have been motivated by a desire to prove that the three companies did do their own manufacturing. It is gratifying that all the evidence uncovered supports this position. Therefore, it can be said without hesitation that Canada Clock Company I, the Hamilton Clock Company and the Canada Clock Company II did manufacture their own cases and movements. In this chapter and the next, evidence is presented in two forms — the written word and a detailed analysis of some of the movements themselves. The evidence is conclusive and establishes the three companies as distinct manufacturers, however much they may have borrowed from contemporary American designs.

THE WRITTEN WORD

One of the frustrating aspects of reviewing the history of the three companies is the scarcity of written records. To date, the authors were unable to uncover any correspondence, price lists or advertising. Contemporary records from newspapers and business journals of the period do exist. The most conclusive evidence that the clocks were made in Canada appears in a series of excerpts from newspapers which are given below. Complete quotations appear in Part I of this book.

ITEM 1:
THE WHITBY CHRONICLE, 6 MARCH 1873
     This lengthy article details the visit of a newspaper correspondent to the factory in Whitby and describes at length the manufacture of movements and cases. The following excerpts are self-explanatory:
     "To those who have never been inside one, the establishment for the manufacture of clocks — where all the parts are made and put together on the spot, is a curious and interesting sight.... But our surprise may be guessed at, when we were informed that not only were all the works made on the premises but all the tools, punches, dies, etc. by the enterprising proprietors themselves.... The building is in two storeys, 100 feet by 50 feet. The first floor is the general workshop and contains all the heavy machinery.... To the left are three costly turning lathes used in making punches, stamps and dies; a large arched adjustable press used for punching and heavy work of the kind and weighing some 30 hundredweight; a friction drop press, a single action press, the latter calculated for

manipulating the finer work. We next come to a wheel cutter, a beautifully finished machine costing alone $1200 and with a capacity of cutting the cogs in 10,000 wheels a day.... Further on there are three of what are called chuck lathes, applied to turning and finishing pinions, centre shafts etc.... In the addition or lean-to, the building on the west side, are the wire rollers and also the chemical apparatus for brightening the works.... Returning through the general workshop we have pointed out to us machines for straightening out coiled wire, rollers for flattening and rolling pendulum wires etc., also an emery wheel for brightening the works — four vices and benches at which workmen are engaged and various other contrivances.

"...The upper storey contains four departments — one for case work, one for veneering and varnishing, a third for polishing and finishing and a well-lighted airy room called the movement room, for putting the works together."

ITEM 2:
THE WHITBY CHRONICLE, 17 JUNE 1875
"The proprietor of the clock factory has just shown us a very ingenious piece of clockwork, manufactured by hand by the celebrated lock and safe maker, Mr. Hennessy of Hamilton.... The instrument has a spring, is wound up like a clock, runs for sixty hours, has a dial that can be set for any time from one to sixty hours... Five hundred of these instruments have been ordered to be manufactured at our Clock Factory and many more will be required...."

ITEM 3:
THE WHITBY CHRONICLE, 25 MAY 1876
"The Clock Factory Going to Hamilton....
A company has been organized in Hamilton with a capital of $100,000 and has purchased the machinery of the clock factory from Colonel Wallace...."

ITEM 4:
THE HAMILTON SPECTATOR, 28 SEPTEMBER 1882
"The Canada Clock Company of Hamilton exhibited fifty-five clocks in forty-three styles and also seven simple movements." This display was shown on the ground floor of the Palace at the Great Central Fair, Hamilton, Ontario.

ITEM 5:
THE CANADIAN MANUFACTURER, 19 OCTOBER 1883
This is a lengthy article from a trade publication and describes in great detail the premises of the Canada Clock Company II in Hamilton. The following excerpts are significant:
"It may be news to many residents of the 'Ambitious City' to learn that the Canada Clock Company... is the only manufacturer of clocks in this broad Dominion.... It is marvellous to take a walk through the various departments in this factory and see to what perfection machinery has been brought, when the delicate works comprising the interior of a clock can all be cut out and shaped by machines with an accuracy which could not possibly be arrived at — except with excessive labour and great loss of time — with tools in the hands of workmen. As it is, however, nothing is thought of turning out two to five thousand clocks of the same size and pattern in which there will not be the slightest flaw or the slightest difference in detail.... It may be said that with the exception of the springs, everything connected with these clocks is manufactured on the premises. This has only, to a great extent, been obtained since the N.P. (National Policy) came into existence, its preventative tariff of 35 percent shutting out the American manufacturer from sending the 'interior economy' of the clocks — so to speak — across the line.... In the machinery room the brass is cut into sizes for the various parts of the movements. Then the plates which hold the parts together are shaped by a punching machine,

which makes a correct plate each time it descends. Here, also, the wheels and pinions are made by ingenious machinery, which is driven at a high rate of speed, one turning lathe being driven at the extraordinarily high speed of 9000 revolutions per minute.... From the machine room the parts are taken to the dipping room, where they are immersed in a strong solution of acids which relieves them of any particles of dust which may be sticking to them and gives them, besides, a polished appearance. In this room, too, the pendulums, dial rims and any other parts requiring it are nickel plated. The parts are taken from here to the movement room, where they are put together in remarkably quick time. In this room a young woman has perhaps the most difficult and certainly the most tedious task in the factory. Her occupation is to pick up short pieces of fine wire with a pair of pincers and force them through the half dozen small holes which keep two of the tiny wheels on the pinion together.... Clock movements would look odd unless enclosed in cases, and this part of the business is consequently a part and parcel of clock manufacture. Various kinds of wood are used for the cases, from pine to mahogany, and, in this department, too, so ably does the machinery do its work that, such things as planes and other tools for smoothing edges are unknown. In some of the elaborate cases, however, carving has to be resorted to, but in ordinary cases the turning machines do the work. When the cases are glued and tacked together they are brought in to the varnish room, where they are first stained and any openings in the wood filled in. They are afterwards varnished and made ready for the glass doors. Many of these doors are handsomely stained and ornamented from designs gotten up in the factory, some of them also being hand-painted.''

ITEM 6:
THE GLOBE, TORONTO, 7 NOVEMBER 1885

The assets of the bankrupt Canada Clock Company II were disposed of in a judicial sale advertised in the *Globe*. The sale notices once again confirmed the existence of clock manufacturing machinery.

"Judicial sale re Canada Clock Company. Tenders will be received by the liquidators, hereinafter named, up to and including the twentieth November, instant, for the purchase of that desirable factory property known as the Clock Factory at Hamilton, Ontario, together with the fixed and moveable machinery therein, including a 46 h.p. Wheelock Engine manfactured by Goldie and McCulloch and complete machinery, tools, dies, wood planers, moulders, shapers, etc. for the manufacture of clocks, clock trimmings and cases.''

Fig. 17 Typical Waterbury 30-hour Ogee Movement.

CHAPTER SIX
MOVEMENTS

AMERICAN INFLUENCE ON MOVEMENT DESIGN

During the period in which the three Canadian companies operated, the American clockmaking industry reigned supreme. The large manufacturers in Connecticut were at the peak of their power. They had perfected mass production and swept away all the old hand-crafted clocks. American clocks were being sold worldwide. Competition was intense and the U.S. companies copied each other shamelessly. It is hardly surprising, therefore, to find that the production output of clocks in Canada during this period followed successful American trends. This can be seen in the design of both movements and cases. Another point which should be noted is that the men who set up and ran the three Canadian companies were not professional clockmakers. They had, perhaps, at best, good mechanical experience. It would seem obvious then, that they would select successful American movements to copy as the most economical and convenient way of getting into business. Greenwood, had had some prior metal-fabricating experience with his sewing machine factory. Little is known of the previous occupation of the Collins brothers, except that John had mechanical training. In the description of the factory operations in the *Whitby Chronicle*, they have been credited with assembling equipment, dies, jigs, fixtures, etc. This equipment was to be used throughout the life of the three companies.

An examination of the movements used by the three Canadian companies at once confirms that the techniques of the American clock manufacturers were carefully copied. The challenging part of the investigation has been to determine who was copied and whether an exact copy was made. Surprisingly little comprehensive information exists on mass-produced American clock movements of this period. Published articles tend to deal with specific subjects. No one as yet appears to have had the courage or the resources to catalogue all the nineteenth century brass movements that can be found in American clocks. The authors, however, were fortunate at an early stage to have made the acquaintance of Dr. Snowden Taylor, who is currently Research Committee Chairman of the National Association of Watch and Clock Collectors (NAWCC). At the time we first talked to Dr. Taylor, he was deeply involved in the preparation of a major survey of the Noble Jerome 30-hour brass weight movement. He was already compiling a complete list of all known makers and the movements found in these clocks.

Dr. Taylor had recognized the existence of ogee movements by both the Hamilton Clock Company and the Canada Clock Company II. He had noted certain similarities when compared with Waterbury Clock Company movements. The authors had the pleasure of an extended correspondence with Dr. Taylor on the subject of these movements. All parties were able to agree that the movements attributed to the three Canadian companies were significantly different from any movements of American manufacture. The authors of this book, of course, were delighted to have confirmation of their own research from such an eminent authority.

It soon became evident that the 30-hour Waterbury movement was indeed the prototype selected by the Collins brothers for use in their Canadian ogee clocks. A detailed comparison of

Fig. 18 Earliest 30-hour Ogee Movement by the Canada Clock Company, Whitby.

Waterbury movements with the ogee movements found in Canada Clock Company I, Hamilton Clock Company and Canada Clock Company II became a major part of our research.

One can only speculate as to whether the Collins brothers simply copied many aspects of the Waterbury design or whether they obtained some sort of licence. Although there is nothing in the written record, the authors are inclined to the view that Collins merely appropriated the design. Waterbury Clock Company held certain patents on clockwork components, but there is no evidence that the original movement was patented in Canada. The Collins brothers, in a small town in rural Ontario, therefore, probably went ahead with very little hesitation. It is worth noting, too, that in 1872 the Waterbury ogee movement had already been in use for some 15 years and there would have been little novelty left in the design. Snowden Taylor has commented, incidently, that the original Waterbury movement was probably designed for the predecessor of Waterbury, the firm of Benedict and Burnham, by no less a person than Chauncey Jerome, the "father" of all ogee clocks. All of which serves to give the Canada Clock movement an interesting if somewhat illegitimate ancestry.

*Fig. 19 30-hour Ogee Movement by the Ansonia Clock Company
used for a brief period at Whitby.*

THE USE OF ANSONIA MOVEMENTS AT WHITBY

Several ogee clocks from the Whitby period are known to contain Ansonia movements. In view of previous claims in this text about Canadian manufacture, this situation requires some comment.

Four distinct labels were used on ogee clocks made at Whitby and these are described in Chapter 8. These labels coincide, approximately, with different events in the short life of the company. The third and fourth labels were issued while James Wallace was "proprietor" and include his name. The third label (with beaver) was used in conjunction with true Whitby movements. The fourth (plain) label occurs in clocks with Ansonia movements. Closer examination of clocks in the fourth group reveals that some of the cases are not completely veneered. The curved ogee section is raw pine with a heavy coating of dark varnish. This would suggest that Ansonia movements were used to complete "end of the line" clocks.

The record confirms that, after the demise of Canada Clock Company I in 1875, Col. Wallace held two sales to dispose of stock. These sales were advertised in the *Whitby Chronicle* of 13 July 1876 and 24 May 1877. In the sale listings, reference is made to the fact that "the greater part" of the movements had been imported from the Ansonia Clock Company in the United States. It is not known precisely when the Ansonia movements were imported by Wallace. Certainly, production at the Whitby factory had come to a full stop because of the fire on 2 December 1875. At some point, it appears that Wallace found himself in possession of a quantity of cases for which he had no movements. In order to salvage what he could, he imported American movements and sold complete clocks.

The Ansonia movements can readily be identified because their plate shape and general configuration are totally different from the ogee movements that were manufactured at Whitby and later at Hamilton. (see Fig. 18 and Fig. 21) This is the only occasion when any evidence has been found of American movements being used by the three Canadian companies.

A SUMMARY OF MOVEMENTS

Clock movements manufactured by the three companies have been itemized in the following pages, followed by a detailed discussion of two representative examples.

CANADA CLOCK COMPANY I, WHITBY, ONTARIO 1872 to 1875
1. 30-hour, time and strike, weight driven. Found only in ogee cases.

Fig. 20 Second 30-hour Ogee Movement from Whitby.
Comparison with movement in Fig. 18 shows
minor evolutionary changes.

No other clock movements have been authenticated to the Whitby period. It is possible that some experimental spring-driven models were made, but no examples have yet come to the authors' attention. The auction notice for Colonel Wallace's disposal sale did make reference to spring-driven movements and 8-day, time and strike, weight movements. However, there are no known examples of these clocks, and according to the sale notice of 1877, they contained Ansonia movements. One large cottage clock with a spring movement and a Whitby label is reported in Burrows, *Canadian Clocks and Clockmakers* and is illustrated in Chapter 10. The authors have not had the opportunity to examine this clock firsthand, but correspondence with the owner has confirmed that it contains a stamped Ansonia movement. Thus, we can only credit the Whitby plant with having made one movement style.

THE HAMILTON CLOCK COMPANY, HAMILTON, ONTARIO 1876 TO 1880
1. 30-hour, time and strike, weight driven. Found only in ogee cases.

Fig. 21 30-hour Ogee Movement, Hamilton Clock Company.
Note similarity to Fig. 20.

2. 30-hour, time only, spring driven. Usually found in small cottage clocks.

Fig. 22 30-hour Time Only Movement, Hamilton Clock Company.

3. 30-Hour, time and strike, spring driven. Commonly found in mantel clocks of all types.

Fig. 23 30-hour Time and Strike Movement, Hamilton Clock Company.

4. 8-day, time and strike, spring driven. Found in mantel clocks and octagonal wall clocks.

Fig. 24 8-day Time and Strike Movement, Hamilton Clock Company.

5. Separate alarm mechanism. Used in both ogee and mantel clocks.

Fig. 25 Alarm Mechanism, Hamilton Clock Company.

Many Hamilton Clock Company movements are stamped "Hamilton Clock Co., Hamilton, Ont." which greatly simplifies identification. A significant number of correct movements, however, bear no such stamp, and it becomes necessary to compare them with known authentic examples to be completely sure.

Some sharp-eyed reader may question the existence of another movement as illustrated in Fig. 34 of the Burrows book. This movement does not have the characteristics of the normal Hamilton Clock Company movement. The clock is currently in the possession of one of the authors and detailed examination has been possible. It is evident that this movement is a later transplant and is not an original Hamilton Clock Company movement. It is unstamped, but is a typical example of a New Haven ogee movement. The mounting board is of incorrect thickness and has been crudely whittled to fit the case. The movement is also equipped with alarm fittings, but there is no evidence that any alarm mechanism had ever been installed in the case. The authors are satisfied that this is a spurious example.

THE CANADA CLOCK COMPANY II, HAMILTON, ONTARIO 1881 TO 1885

1. 30-hour, time, strike, weight driven. Found only in ogee cases.

Fig. 26 30-hour Ogee Movement, Canada Clock Company II
Major changes are evident when this movement
is compared with Fig. 21.

2. 30-hour, time only, spring driven. Normally found in small cottage clocks. May be installed in "straight-up" or "slant" position.

Fig. 27 30-hour Time Only Movement, Canada Clock Company II.

3. 30-hour, time and alarm, spring driven. Alarm mechanism is installed between the plates of the movement. This movement is frequently found in small cottage clocks.

Fig. 28 30-hour Time and Alarm Movement, Canada Clock Company II. Alarm between plates.

4. 30-hour, time and strike, spring driven. Commonly found in mantel clocks.

Fig. 29 30-hour Time and Strike Movement, Canada Clock Company II.

5. 8-day, time only, spring driven. Found in octagonal and other wall clocks. May also be equipped with additional calendar hand mechanism in octagonal wall clocks.

Fig. 31 8-day Time Only Movement showing Calendar Mechanism, Canada Clock Company II.

Fig. 30 8-day Time Only Movement, Canada Clock Company II.

6. 8-day, time and strike, spring driven. Found in mantel clocks. Occasionally this movement is used in octagonal wall clocks and may be equipped with additional calendar hand mechanism.

Fig. 32 8-day Time and Strike Movement showing Calendar Mechanism, Canada Clock Company II.

Fig. 33 8-day Time and Strike Movement, Canada Clock Company II. This example shows alarm dial.

7. Separate alarm mechanism. Found in some mantel and ogee cases.

Fig. 34 Separate Alarm Mechanism, Canada Clock Company II.

DETAILED MOVEMENT ANALYSIS

Two movements made by the Canadian companies have been selected for detailed study. The first of these is the 30-hour ogee weight-driven movement that was manufactured by all three companies. The second is the 8-day, time and strike spring driven movement, the most elaborate made by these companies, and made during the days of the Hamilton Clock Company and the Canada Clock Company II. No attempt has been made thus far to research the prototypes and ancestry of the other types of movements found in clocks. We will confine ourselves in this chapter simply to describing and illustrating these other movements.

THE 30 HOUR OGEE WEIGHT DRIVEN MOVEMENT

Detailed comparisons have been carried out on typical ogee movements found in clocks made by the Waterbury Clock Company and by the three Canadian companies. A summary of this data is provided in Tables 1a and 1b at the end of this chapter. For purposes of the narrative, however, the differences and exceptions which have been found will be commented upon.

These are summarized as follows:

1. One difference immediately evident is that, in the Canadian clock movements, the plates were held together by four brass nuts. The Waterbury examples examined were all held together with pins inserted through holes in the ends of the posts.

2. There are minor variations in the shape of the click pawl. Clicks used by Waterbury and Canada Clock Company I both have the characteristic "comma" shape. However, the width of the "tail" of the comma varied. Waterbury clicks were were 3/32 inch while the Whitby clicks were 1/8 inch wide. The Hamilton Clock Company changed the shape of the click to something that resembled a keyhole.

3. The mounting pin for the verge is riveted to the front plate in all clocks. However, in Waterbury movements, the pin is situated to the left of the escape wheel in approximately the "11 o'clock" position. All Canadian clocks have the pin mounted to the right in approximately the "2 o'clock" position.

4. The total length of the Waterbury fly was 1 7/8 inches. The fly varied in the Canadian clocks but was never less than 2 1/16 inches and occasionally was as long as 2¼ inches.

5. It is in the plate dimensions themselves that the most significant differences exist. These differences indicate clearly that plates made by Canada Clock Company I, Hamilton Clock Company and Canada Clock Company II could not have been struck by the same dies as those of the Waterbury Clock Company. It is evident that the Canadian clock companies did not change their plate dies during the 14 years of their existence. Measurements of the plates from the three companies show that the dimensions are constant.

In Table 1b, the dimensions in question are detailed. In this data, it can be seen that the outside measurements of the Waterbury plates differ by approximately 1/32 inches (or .031 inches). The "cut out" dimensions also differ by from .010 to .015 inches. During the entire 14-year life of the Canadian companies, in contrast, plate dimensions of their own movements varied by no more than .003 inches. These basic differences between the Canadian and Waterbury clocks confirm the use of different dies. This information also confirms the eyewitness accounts of clock manufacturing both in Whitby and in Hamilton.

Several other comments can be made from the data presented in Table 1b.

1. During the Whitby period, two minor variations can be seen in the ogee movements. Clocks with the "Greenwood" label contain nuts which are 1/8 inch thick. In clocks that have the "no name" label, the nuts are 3/32 inches thick. There is also a variation in the position of the escapement bridge. The "Greenwood" clocks have the bridge placed at a 3 o'clock position relative to the escape wheel, whereas in "no name" clocks, the bridge is located at a 4 o'clock position. The 3 o'clock position was used in all later clocks. Thus, it can be assumed that the 4 o'clock position and the thin nuts were used for a brief period during the early days of the plant corresponding to the "no name" label. (See Fig. 18 and Fig. 20)

Otherwise, there is close similarity between movements from the Canada Clock Company I and the Hamilton Clock Company. The minor differences that were observed seem to be simple running changes.

2. The ogee movements of Canada Clock Company II, made in Hamilton after 1881, have significant differences. The movement underwent a major redesign, and while the same plate dies were used, the other characteristics of the movement are noticeably different. There are significant variations in the number of spokes in the wheels. Most of the wheels now have five spokes rather than the six found previously and as found in Waterbury movements. The escape wheel now has only four spokes. (See Fig. 26)

It is evident that after recapitalization in 1881 and the formation of Canada Clock Company II, money was spent to modernize the movements. The new ogee movement now contained a feature that allowed the minute hand to be turned backward past 12 o'clock without damage to the striking mechanism. This feature is frequently mentioned on the labels of the period. It is of interest to note that certain Waterbury clocks of the same era had a similar device. Some of the latter clocks also contain the information, "Patented September 22, 1874." Through the research facilities of the NAWCC, the authors were able to obtain a copy of U.S. Patent No. 155,244, "Lifting Hooks for Striking Clocks," dated 22 September 1874 and assigned to John Connor, inventor. The patent describes exactly the device that the Canada Clock Company II began to use in 1881 to allow hands to be turned back. There is no reference anywhere on the labels to a patent in Canada and it seems evident that, again, Canada Clock Company II took advantage of American technology and merely copied it.

3. Another obvious difference which exists in the 1881 Canadian movement involved the rearrangement of the second wheel in the time train. This wheel was reversed in its positioning so that the large gear was now located at the back of the movement and the pinion was to the front. There is no immediately obvious reason for this change.

4. Another change in the latter movement involved the occasional use of wheel-stiffening rings that had not been seen previously in any of the companies' movements.

THE 8-DAY TIME AND STRIKE SPRING DRIVEN MOVEMENT

The 8-day time and strike movement (see Figs. 24 & 33) appears in clocks made both by Hamilton Clock Company and Canada Clock Company II. The movement has never been seen in clocks of Whitby origin. When the Canada Clock Company II and the Hamilton Clock Company movements are compared with those of American manufacture, there is once again a very close resemblance to the 8-day time and strike movement found in American clocks of the period.

In the following pages, some of the similarities and differences will be outlined. Before starting a detailed comparison, it must be pointed out that at least four American companies manufactured similar movements in the same general time period. Examples of the basic 8-day time and strike design have been found in clocks by Waterbury, Ansonia, Atkins and E.N. Welch. In each case, there is a close similarity in plate shape and wheel configuration, but many differences in more minor details. Certainly, it is beyond the scope of this study to trace the origins of movement development in the U.S.A., but it is again obvious that there was much copying. The Canadian companies seem content to have done likewise.

The Canadian movements differ in many respects from all four American counterparts. This study has concentrated on Waterbury as the probable prototype, but illustrations of the other three U.S. movements are included. (See Figs. 36 to 38)

Tables 2a and 2b have been prepared to compare Waterbury movements with those of Hamilton Clock Company and Canada Clock Company II. The most important differences can be summarized as follows:

1. The Canada Clock Company II and the Hamilton Clock Company have used brass nuts to hold plates together, whereas the Waterbury Clock Company has used blued steel screws. The illustration of the Ansonia movement also indicates the use of screws.

The following illustrations show American movements with characteristics similar to the 8-day time and strike movement made by Hamilton Clock Company and Canada Clock Company II.

Fig. 35 Waterbury 8-day, Time and Strike Movement.

Fig. 36 Ansonia 8-day, Time and Strike Movement. From 1880 Catalogue.

Fig. 37 Atkins 8-day, Time and Strike Movement.

Fig. 38 E.N. Welch 8-day, Time and Strike Movement.

2. The mounting post for the pendulum suspension spring is situated below the central arbour in all known examples of the Canadian companies. Waterbury and Ansonia both appear to have used a position around 2 o'clock above and to the right of the central arbour.

3. Differences can be seen in many of the minor parts of the movement when comparing the Waterbury versus the Canadian version. Examples include the shape of the click pawl, the escape wheel bridge, the verge retaining wire and the feet for mounting the movement to the case. Two of the seven examples in Table 2a contain separate alarm mechanisms. It can be seen that the shape of the triggering levers and the alarms themselves are quite different when comparing the Canada Clock Company II with the Waterbury Clock Company.

4. Comments were made previously on the observable differences in the ogee movement after 1881. Certain changes appear to have taken place in the 8-day spring movement as well. One sees that no longer are all wheels made with six spokes. The movements contain both four- and five-spoke wheels, although it is somewhat difficult to figure out the rationale with which the change was made.

5. The size of the brass hubs that are attached to the plate at the number one wheel of the Canadian and Waterbury movements have different dimensions. Likewise, there are minor variations in the placement of oil sinks on the front plate. Waterbury also riveted the count wheel washer to the front plate, whereas the Canadian makers have allowed this washer to run loose. Other differences that are outlined in Table 3 appear to represent discretionary changes that could have been made from month to month during the operation of the plant.

6. It is interesting to consider the use of the "turn hands back" mechanisms in the Canada Clock Company II, 8-day movements. As commented previously in this chapter, this mechanism was an American patent utilized by the Waterbury Clock Company after 1874. Examples of the "turn hands back" mechanism appear in the Canadian clocks after 1881. The device itself is a small triangular attachment that has been set into the main arbour. (See Fig. 39) This allows the signal wire for the strike mechanism to be deflected harmlessly when the hands are turned backwards. Prior to this patent, most American clock manufacturers employed an L-shaped wire or "unlocking pin" set into the main arbour that lifted a wire "unlocking hook." However, when the arbour was turned backwards, the L-shaped device became fouled in the unlocking hook and damage could result. This L-shaped wire is found in the 8-day time and strike movement of the Hamilton Clock Company. Canada Clock Company II evidently appropriated the patent for its own use and reference is made to the device in their labels. No reference is made to the patent, however. It was surprising to find in one "Prince of Wales" model that someone had attempted to use a device which would get around the Waterbury patent. This consisted of a hinge that was attached to the main arbour. This hinge would remain in the erect position when the hands were moving forward. However, when the hands were turning backwards, the hinge folded down out of the way and allowed the unlocking hook to go past without damage. This has only been found in one clock. It is impossible to determine whether it was an experimental device installed at the plant or was the result of some subsequent repair job. Hopefully, it represents an attempt on the part of the Canada Clock Company II to devise their own turnback device. If this were the case, they obviously concluded that it was cheaper and easier to copy the Waterbury device once again.

Another strike variation occurs in several 8-day movements. This consists of a half-hour strike. Most clocks made by the three companies struck only the hour. However, a few of the more elaborate case styles by Canada Clock Company II are equipped with the half-hour mechanism. Involved is a simple wire hook fixed to the strike hammer arbour. The hook is activated by the same unlocking pin on the main arbour which activates the hourly strike.

In these clocks the unlocking pin is the simple bent wire variety as shown in Fig. 39-Type I. Thus the hands cannot be turned back past 12 o'clock.

The data presented in Tables 2a and 2b parallel the data that was accumulated for the ogee movement. The plate shape again is similar to that of the Waterbury Clock Company, but the actual dimensions are significantly different in almost every instance. The c, d, and e dimensions vary as much as .025 inches between the two companies, and it is evident, once again, that different dies were used to prepare the plates.

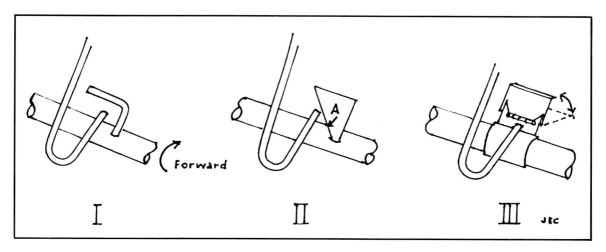

Fig. 39 Sketch of 3 "turn hands back" mechanisms.
I. As used by Hamilton Clock Company. Cannot turn hands back.
II. Connors (Waterbury) Patent. Used by Canada Clock Company II.
Bevel 'A' pushes wire aside when hands reversed.
III. Hinged device found on one Canada Clock Company II clock.

To conclude the remarks on the 8-day movement, it is apparent again that the Hamilton Clock Company and the Canada Clock Company II did indeed manufacture their own movements. While the resemblance to the movements of American companies is unmistakable, the differences are significantly numerous and of such a nature that there is no doubt that the movements are of Canadian manufacture.

OTHER MOVEMENTS OF CANADIAN MANUFACTURE

Table 3 at the end of this chapter contains the mechanical characteristics of the other movements, but no effort has been made to compare them with the movements of American manufacture.

1. 30-hour, time only, spring driven

These little movements are found in cottage clocks and other small timepieces manufactured by both the Hamilton Clock Company and the Canada Clock Company II. Comments were made previously on the use of nuts to secure the plates in the ogee and 8-day movements. It is interesting to note that in many of the smaller movements, nuts were not employed. The plates were held in place by tapered pins or bent wires inserted through holes in the ends of the posts. These movements are not stamped by the manufacturer. This is probably due to the fact that the stamp was larger than any clear area on these small plates. A few running changes can be seen in the movement as the company evolved. This is particularly noticeable in the spoke count of the escape wheel. The earlier Hamilton clocks have six spokes and the later Canada Clock Company II clocks have four spokes. One other interesting development took place during the days of the Canada Clock Company II. The movement can be found mounted in a "straight-up" or "slant" position.

This situation perplexed the authors. However, a very simple explanation was suggested by Snowden Taylor. He observed that, if the movement were mounted on a slant, the pendulum then hung exactly in the middle of the case. When the movement is installed in the "straight-up" position, the pendulum is decidedly off centre. It is evident that the use of the "slant" position was merely to improve the appearance of the clocks. The "straight-up" position was more often used during the time of the Hamilton Clock Company. Both positions were used by the Canada Clock Company II. The other inevitable consequence of mounting the movement on a slant is that the position of the winding arbour is changed. The "straight-up" movements always have a winding opening at 11 on the dial, while the winding arbour of the "slant" movement ends up at 10. Although this movement is time only, it is occasionally found in clocks that are equipped with a separate alarm. Examples of this can be seen in clocks made by both the Hamilton companies. The illustrations in Chapter 10 show most of these variations.

Fig. 40 Two Cottage Clocks by Canada Clock Company II showing movements installed in "straight-up" and "slant" positions.

2. 30-hour, time and alarm

The 30-hour time and alarm movement was made during the time of Canada Clock Company II at Hamilton. It is a simple 30-hour movement with the alarm device mounted between the plates on the left-hand side of the movement. The alarm is set in a manner similar to that used in most American clocks of the period. The alarm is controlled by a small brass dial which is mounted on the central arbour and which protrudes through an opening in the face. To set the alarm, the little dial is twisted until the desired hour lies under the hour hand. The spring is then wound by a key and the alarm will go off at the correct time. This time and alarm mechanism is found in a few small mantel and cottage clocks. It is commonly found in the small "City of Paris" model. (See Fig. 122)

Fig. 41 This Waterbury 30-hour Time Only Movement may have been the prototype for Figs. 22 and 27 (not researched in text).

3. 30-hour, time and strike, spring driven

30-hour spring-driven movements are found in both the Hamilton Clock Company and Canada Clock Company II clocks. 30-hour time and strike clocks appear to have been popular and many examples are found from each company. It is interesting to note, however, that the Hamilton Clock Company movement is totally different from the Canada Clock Company II movement. The reason for the change is unknown, but it was evidently part of the general reorganization that took place in 1881. The movement used by the Hamilton Clock Company is a fairly simple design with rectangular plates. It bears some resemblance to the 30-hour time and strike movements used in this period by the Ansonia Clock Company (The Ansonia Brass & Copper Company) although the two movements are by no means identical. The later movement used by the Canada Clock Company II had changed completely in its plate shape and the configuration of its wheels. Both movements, as usual, are held together by brass nuts. The Hamilton Clock Company movement was mounted with wooden blocks. This practice was used in most of the larger movements by the Hamilton Clock Company. The Canada Clock Company II movement is mounted on steel feet held to the case by screw nails. (See Fig. 23, Hamilton Clock Company and Fig. 29 Canada Clock Company II.)

4. 8-day, time only, spring driven

This movement has been found in wall clocks manufactured by Canada Clock Company II. It is a simple, basic time only movement with wind-up hole at 7 o'clock. The plates are rectangular and a variety of four-, five- and six-spoked wheels is used. The movement is used in both the octagonal "Schoolhouse" clocks and the round-bottomed "Regulator" model.

The calendar mechanism can be seen in Fig. 31. This mechanism was fitted to both 8-day time only and time and strike movements.

While commenting on wall clocks, it is worth mentioning that octagonal wall clocks manufactured by the Hamilton Clock Company appear to have been equipped only with the 8-day time and strike movement. The escape wheel was modified to accommodate the longer drop. Octagonal wall clocks by the Canada Clock Company II were equipped with several movement variations, including time only; time and strike; time and calendar; and, time, strike and calendar. The "Regulator" wall clock by Canada Clock Company II has been seen with time only and time and strike movements.

One transitional 8-day time, strike and calendar octagonal wall clock is known. The movement is stamped Hamilton Clock Company, but it is installed in a labelled case by Canada Clock Company II. (See Fig. 159)

Fig. 42 Octagonal Wall Clock by Hamilton Clock Company with 8-day Time and Strike Movement.

*Fig. 43 Two "Regulators" by Canada Clock Company II
showing Two Movement Options.*

5. Separate Alarm Mechanism

The separate alarm mechanism is found in clocks manufactured by both the Hamilton Clock Company and the Canada Clock Company II. No evidence was found that any were used during the Whitby period. The devices are found both in ogee weight clocks and in spring-driven mantel clocks. Examples have been seen of almost every movement type coupled to a separate alarm. Some minor variations were noted in the separate alarms examined: some have three feet, some have four; some have stop work, some do not, etc. The general appearance of the mechanism resembles those used by the New Haven Clock Company, Connecticut, but again are not identical. There are variations in openings, foot design, etc. These little movements do not share any parts with the regular clock movements, therefore it is difficult to state whether or not they were manufactured in Canada.

WHEEL COUNT

The information provided in Table 3, at the end of this chapter, gives further evidence of movement changes which were carried out before the start-up of the Canada Clock Company II in 1881. The most noticeable was replacement of the 30-hour, spring-driven time and strike movement, as made by the Hamilton Clock Company. The new movement was completely different in both plate shape and gearing.

Three other changes have been noted. The first affected the 30-hour time only movement — a result of its being installed in both "straight-up" and "slant" positions. In the slant position, a longer pendulum rod was used in order to keep the "bob" at the previous level. This necessitated a decrease in teeth of the third wheel from 54 to 48. Some modifications were also made in the strike train of the 8-day striking mechanism. This change may have provided some benefit but, a century later, after many years of wear, both configurations are capable of eccentric behaviour. Comment has already been made on the reversing of certain wheels and pinions in the ogee movement after 1881. It is interesting to note, however, that no changes were made in the wheel and pinion counts in any of the three basic ogee movements.

30-HOUR OGEE MOVEMENTS
Table 1A Plate Dimensions

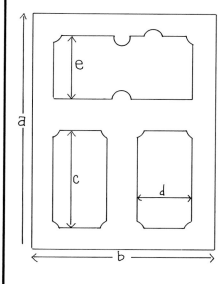

	a	b	c	d	e
Waterbury	4.63″	3.53″	0.970″	1.962″	1.310″
* Canada I (A)	4.59″	3.56″	0.960″	1.947″	1.297″
** Canada I (B)	4.59″	3.56″	0.960″	1.950″	1.296″
Hamilton	4.59″	3.56″	0.960″	1.948″	1.296″
Canada II	4.59″	3.56″	0.961″	1.949″	1.296″

* First Movement (No place name label)
** Second Movement (Greenwood Collins label)

30-HOUR OGEE MOVEMENTS
—Table 1B Mechanical Differences—

	Waterbury	Canada I (A)	Canada I (B)	Hamilton	Canada II
Plates Held By	Steel Pins	Brass Nuts	Brass Nuts	Brass Nuts	Brass Nuts
Click Shape	0.095″	0.125″	0.125″		
Position of Verge Pin Mount					
Escapement Bridge, Rivets Etc.	Curved	Straight			
Count Wheel Washer Rivetted?	Yes	Yes	Yes	No	No
Second Wheel Time Train	Toward Front of Movement	Toward Front	Toward Front	Toward Front	Toward Rear

8-DAY TIME & STRIKE MOVEMENTS
Table 2A Plate Dimensions

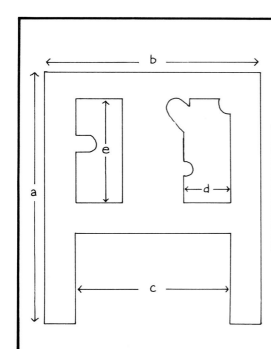

	a	b	c	d	e
Waterbury 1874	5.19″	3.494″	2.303″	0.865″	2.523″
Hamilton A	5.20″	3.494″	2.325″	0.846″	2.495″
Hamilton B	5.20″	3.493″	2.322″	0.844″	2.493″
Canada II A	5.20″	3.503″	2.323″	0.847″	2.496″
Canada II B	5.20″	3.499″	2.319″	0.846″	2.496″
Canada II C	5.20″	3.498″	2.318″	0.845″	2.497″
Canada II R	5.20″	3.497″	Damaged	0.844″	2.496″

NOTE: Hamilton A & B were Standard Mantle Clocks. Canada II A, B & C were "Prince of Wales", "Ontario" & "Victoria" Models, respectively. Canada II "R" was "Regulator" Wall Clock.

8-DAY TIME & STRIKE MOVEMENTS
Table 2B Mechanical Differences

	Waterbury 1874 Pat.	Hamilton A	Hamilton B	Canada II A	Canada II B	Canada II C	Canada II R
Plates Held By	Blued Steel Screws	Brass Nuts	Brass Nuts	Brass Nuts	Brass Nuts	Brass Nuts	Brass Nuts
Click Shape							
Turn Hands Back? Mechanism	Yes	No	No	Yes (Hinge)	Yes	Yes	No
Escape Wheel Bridge	Curved	Straight	Same As Hamilton "A"		Same As Canada II "A"	Same As Canada II "A"	Same As Canada II "A"
Count Wheel Washer Rivetted?	Yes	No	No	No	No	No	No
Pendulum Suspension Post	Above Center Arbor	Below	Below	Below	Below	Below	Below
Escape Wheel Cut-Out, Front Plate			Same As Hamilton "A"	Same As Hamilton "A"	Same As Hamilton "A"	Same As Hamilton "A"	Same As Hamilton "A"
Shape of Verge Retaining Wire							
Unlocking Bar For Separate Alarm	Rivet 0.375″	Not Present	Not Present	Screw 0.250″	Not Present	Not Present	Not Present

TABLE 3 WHEEL COUNTS

Time Train	Canada Clock Co.I (Whitby, Ont.)	HAMILTON CLOCK CO. (HAMILTON, ONT.)			
	30-Hr. Time & Strike Weight (OGEE)	30-Hr. Time & Strike Weight (OGEE)	30-Hr. Time Only Spring	30-Hr. Time & Strike Spring	8-Day Time & Strike Spring
No. 1 Wheel	78	78	50	78	84
No. 2 Pinion Wheel	6 80	6 80	6 48	7 50	8 60
No. 3 Pinion Wheel	—	—	6 * 54	6 42	8 40
No. 4 Pinion Wheel	—	—	—	—	7 40
Escape Pinion Wheel	6 42	6 42	6 44	6 42	7 * 42
Comment			* Movement mounted straight up		* Wall Clock = 34 Large Mantle = 39
Strike Train					
No. 1 Wheel	78	78	—	78	84
No. 2 Pinion Wheel	6 80	6 80	—	5 48	7 52
No. 3 Pinion Wheel	—	—	—	6 56	6 48
Fly Pinion	5	5	—	5	6
Comment					

TABLE 3 WHEEL COUNTS (CONT.)
CANADA CLOCK CO. II (HAMILTON, ONT.)

Time Train	30-Hr. Time & Strike Weight (OGEE)	30-Hr. Time Only Spring	30-Hr. Time & Alarm Spring	30-Hr. Time & Strike Spring	8-Day Time Only Spring	8-Day Time & Strike Spring
No. 1 Wheel	78	50	50	74	84	84
No. 2 Pinion Wheel	6 80	6 48	6 48	7 48	8 60	8 60
No. 3 Pinion Wheel	—	6 * 48	6 48	6 40	8 40	8 40
No. 4 Pinion Wheel	—	—	—	—	7 40	7 40
Escape Pinion Wheel	6 42	6 ** 44	6 42	6 40	7 34	7 * 40
Comment		* Slant Mount 48 Straight Mount 54 ** Large Cottage = 42				* Wall Clock = 34
Strike Train						
No. 1 Wheel	78	—	40	74	—	84
No. 2 Pinion Wheel	6 80	—	7 * 24	6 54	—	7 52
No. 3 Pinion Wheel	—	—	—	6 50	—	6 64
Fly Pinion	5	—	—	6	—	7
Comment			* No. 2 Wheel is alarm escapement			

CHAPTER SEVEN
CASE STYLES

In Part I, the authors quoted all the articles that were found in newspapers and journals concerning the Canada Clock Company I, Whitby, and the Canada Clock Company II, Hamilton. These references not only describe the manufacture of movements at both factories, but also present clear evidence of the existence of woodworking machinery and the manufacture of cases. It is reasonable to assume, therefore, that the cases used by all three Canadian companies were of their own manufacture. During the 12 years of their existence, definite changes of policy occurred, so it is not surprising that there are some distinctive changes in case design that can be related to each period. In this chapter, an attempt has been made to analyse the styling trends that were characteristic for each company.

Comments on the American influence on movement design were made previously. The worldwide success of cheap mass-produced clocks from Connecticut certainly made its influence felt in the design of cases as well. It is encouraging to note, however, that from time to time, distinctive clocks were made by the Canadian companies, indicating that some independent thinking had occurred. Case styles for each company are discussed below.

THE CANADA CLOCK COMPANY I, WHITBY

Only a small number of case styles was used during the Whitby period. By far the largest number of cases appears to have been those used for the simple 30-hour ogee weight-driven clocks. Although there were some label variations, there was no change in style or dimension. All clock cases examined are approximately 15 3/8 inches wide, 26 7/8 inches high and 4 inches deep. These proportions correspond closely to competitive American cases of the same period. It is difficult to make exact comparisons because there seem to be almost as many American case sizes as there were manufacturers. However, the Canadian ogee cases were intended to be a "close copy" of the American cases. In one of the Whitby newspaper articles, some reference was made to the use of superior wood. There seems to be some justification for this observation because some of the early ogees of the Whitby period did contain excellent "crotch" mahogany veneers. In the opinion of the authors, these veneers were definitely superior to some of the straight-grained woods used in the U.S.A., although it is fair to state that American companies, such as Ansonia, used superior veneers from time to time.

The only other documented case style from the Whitby period is a large, square cottage clock with a tiger maple base. This clock is illustrated in Fig. 88 and Fig. 89. It appears to be similar in style characteristics to later clocks made by the Hamilton Clock Company. As John Collins worked in both companies, it may well have been a prototype design.

There are some unanswered questions about case styles supposedly made in Whitby. Reference has already been made to the auction sales of surplus clocks held by Colonel Wallace in 1876 and 1877. A number of case styles was listed for sale although none of these has been documented by actual examination. Mention was made in the sale notices of "Octagon Prize" clocks, regulators, 8-day calendar spring strike clocks, 8-day calendar (large), hall and dining room clocks, etc. It was also evident that the woodworking shop in the Whitby factory had attempted the manufacture of other wooden items. The auction sale notices make reference to shawl and lace boxes, knife and spoon boxes, picture and looking-glass frames, etc.

It is impossible to say how many of the wooden items were made by the Canada Clock Company I. However, some further references should be made to the "Octagon Prize" clocks. Initially it was assumed that these were octagonal wall clocks. However, examination of American clock company catalogues of this period reveals that the term "Octagon Prize" is frequently used to describe a "four-sided top" mantel clock. At least four different models of Octagon Prize mantel clocks are illustrated in the New Haven Clock Company catalogue for 1880. This case style was also used by the Hamilton Clock Company.

Apparently, few if any of the clocks offered at auction have survived. Possibly they were never labelled. It has also been suggested that the stock was bought out by the Hamilton Clock Company, which already owned the machinery from Whitby, and the cases incorporated into their regular production. This, however, is only conjecture.

THE HAMILTON CLOCK COMPANY

The new company offered a much wider variety of clocks than the Canada Clock Company I. They continued to produce the 30-hour, weight-driven ogee clocks. In addition, they offered spring-driven clocks in two sizes of cottage clock cases, two sizes of steeple clocks, a variety of 30-hour and 8-day mantel clocks, a drop octagon wall clock, and a very limited number of higher quality, hand-carved walnut mantel clocks. Since all these clocks are relatively rare, it is possible that additional case styles were sold and have not yet been reported.

The ogee cases manufactured by the Hamilton Clock Company were identical to those made by the Canada Clock Company I. The dimensions are exactly the same — 15 3/8 inches wide, 25 7/8 inches high and 4 inches deep. (See Figs. 91, 92, 93)

The cottage clocks were simple little timepieces having 30-hour time only movements, occasionally with separate alarm. The smaller size was approximately 9½ inches tall. The cases examined appear to be made of solid pine stained to a dark colour. The large cottage clocks stood approximately 12½ inches tall. The single specimen examined was made of solid walnut. Illustrations of these clocks can be seen in Chapter 10.

When one examines the 30-hour and 8-day mantel clocks, a considerable variety of case styles is found, but they are all constructed from a limited number of components. All the case construction seems to have been done in pine. A final decorative finish was usually provided in mahogany veneer. There are, however, a small number of these clocks that can be found with no veneer. A simulated woodgrain finish has been applied instead to the wood and stained dark to resemble walnut or mahogany. By the ingenious use of two simple moulding styles and two different bases, a wide variety of mantel clock cases was manufactured. The most common base measured 4 5/8 inches by 11 3/8 inches. Its total height was 1¾ inches. It included a double ogee curve. The second base was slightly smaller, measuring 4 3/8 inches by 10½ inches. The overall height was 2 inches and the base included a single radius curve at the top. The moulding that was used to form the sides and top of the case was a simple shape with a curved front section. The curved portion measured either 1 inch or 1½ inch in width. By suitable use of mitred corners, this moulding was assembled to provide either a square top, a steeple top, or a four-sided "octagon prize" top. Almost all of the permutations of shape, moulding width and base construction can be found in Chapter 10.

Additional case style variations were obtained by the use of either round brass dial pans or simple painted sheet zinc faces which were cut to fit. Perhaps the most common case style was the four-sided top or octagon prize shape. This would lend some credence to the theory that the octagon prize clocks left over from the Whitby factory were eventually absorbed by the Hamilton Clock Company.

The superior quality mantel clocks mentioned earlier and illustrated in Fig. 107 and Fig. 108 are of considerable interest because they contain extensive amounts of hand carving and are different in style from American clocks of the period. They included some extra features, such as glass panels in the sides, and were obviously intended to sell for a higher price. The two examples are similar to one another except that they are mounted on different base styles. They appear to be the only specimens attempted by the Hamilton Clock Company in the deluxe category.

Mention has been made of a drop octagon wall clock that was available from the Hamilton Clock Company. This clock bore a considerable resemblance to clocks offered by the New Haven Clock Company of this period. The basic case was constructed of pine with an overlay of rosewood veneer. (Fig. 109)

A further mention should be made of the two sizes of steeple or "gothic" clock styles. These are almost certainly the only commercial steeple clocks ever to have been made in Canada. They are extremely rare, the small steeple clock in Fig. 104 being the only reported specimen. Both sizes of clocks bear a family resemblance to American steeple clocks of the period. However, there are some individual differences. The small steeple clock is made of tiger maple, rarely used in mass-produced American clocks. The larger clocks are constructed with both the single and double curved base forms. American clocks do not have bases that are exactly the same as those of the Canadian clocks.

Finally, the readers' attention is directed to Fig. 110. This charming little clock appears to have been a "special." The front is a single piece of walnut, hand shaped with a jig saw. On the back is a large and unique label that names the clock the "Simpson." This is the only known clock by the Hamilton Clock Company to be given a model name — and it is named after the company's president! Only one specimen has been seen.

THE CANADA CLOCK COMPANY II, HAMILTON, ONTARIO

A major reorganization took place in the factory in 1881, as previously noted. At that time, George Lee and John Collins left the company and new investors were found with additional capital. The new company, The Canada Clock Company Ltd., was set up as a limited liability company.

The new management obviously decided to take a more aggressive approach to the marketing of clocks in Canada. As a consequence, there were changes and additions to the line of movements and a great profusion of new case styles. One can readily believe the *Hamilton Spectator* article in 1882 which reported that the Canada Clock Company was exhibiting 43 different case styles and seven simple movements. Some further evidence of the activity in this period can be gleaned from the 1883 report of the *Canadian Manufacturer* which refers to 50 employees. *Dun's Mercantile Report* of July 1884 states that the Canada Clock Company at that time had a subscribed capital of $42,000. This would have been a substantial company in 1884, with a well-equipped factory.

Chapter 10 provides illustrations of all known styles of clocks manufactured by Canada Clock Company II and the variety of designs speaks for itself. The company made some fundamental changes in its case styling when compared with the Hamilton Clock Company. The first change was to do away entirely with the process of veneering. The authors have not seen any clocks made by Canada Clock II that had veneered cases. Secondly, the simple and standardized case components used by the Hamilton Clock Company were also abandoned. In their place, clock cases were made of solid woods — walnut, mahogany, butternut and pine — with a good deal of machine work, either turning or carving. These changes were an obvious attempt to keep up with changing American tastes during the 1880s.

Cases made by the Canada Clock Company II can be discussed in several groups.

OGEE CLOCKS

The old reliable 30-hour ogee clock continued to be a popular seller. However, some fairly radical changes were made in construction compared with the output of the two previous companies. The wood was no longer veneered. Instead, pine and butternut were used to build the case and colouring was applied by a sponge or other means to simulate fine wood. The front and sides of the case were usually made of butternut and the back boards of pine. The door frame itself was made of butternut. The mouldings used to form the door included a small, decorative beaded edge, giving the door a quite distinctive appearance. This combination of woods, simulated veneer and decorative trim is completely unique to the Canada Clock Company II. No other ogee clocks, either in Canada or the U.S.A., are known to have this feature. The use of butternut is interesting as well. This is not a common wood in clock case construction, but was popular with the Canada Clock Company II.

COTTAGE CLOCKS

A variety of small 30-hour cottage clocks was offered by Canada Clock Company II. Styles ranged from very simple, square boxes resembling German clocks of the period to fairly elaborate cases. Names such as "Montreal Cottage Clock" and "Metropolitan" were used. These cases average 9½ inches to 10 inches in height. A second line of larger cases for cottage clocks was also offered. These cases were 12½ inches to 13 inches in height and sometimes included ornamental top rails. The small cottage clocks were normally equipped either with 30-hour time only or 30-hour time and alarm movement with the alarm installed between the plates. The larger cottage clocks sometimes had 30-hour time and strike movements and, occasionally, a separate alarm.

MANTEL CLOCKS

A wide array of cases for mantel clocks was manufactured, ranging in height from approximately 14 inches to over 24 inches. The styles varied from very simple, boxy clocks, such as the "Montefiori," to elaborate side-mirrored clocks like the "Victoria." This side-mirrored or "Jenny Lind" clock was obviously the top of the line and was named appropriately after the reigning monarch. Many of the case styles were original designs by the Canada Clock Company staff, but it is also fair to state that others were obvious copies of popular American clocks. Models that appear to be original in design include "Montefiori," "Hero," "Windsor," "Forest Beauty," "City of Paris," etc. A cursory examination of clocks offered in the catalogues of American companies in the 1880s suggests that the Canada Clock Company II staff copied case styles offered by New Haven, Waterbury and Ansonia companies. For example, the New Haven "Neva" served as a model for the "Winnipeg." The Canada Clock Company model "St. Lawrence" is similar to the New Haven "Rhine" and the "Golden Light," Fig. 147, is similar to the New Haven "Apollo." It can be seen that the Canada Clock Company's "Prince of Wales" bears a close resemblance to the Ansonia "King." However, close inspection of the two clocks indicates many small differences that could have occurred when someone copied the original.

There is a very close resemblance between the Canada Clock Company II "Victoria" and both the New Haven "Occidental" and the Ansonia "Triumph." In fact, these so-called "Jenny Lind" cases, by several contemporary manufacturers, are so similar that one is tempted to wonder if they all came from some central source.

It must be remembered, of course, that the Canada Clock Company II had a well-equipped wood-working shop and could have copied any designs effectively, in addition to creating its own material.

Illustrations of all these clocks are included in Chapter 10.

WALL CLOCKS

Since only two basic models of wall clocks were identified, this can be a fairly short discussion. The octagonal clock offered by both the Hamilton Clock Company and Canada Clock Company II bears a close resemblance to the New Haven "Drop Octagon R.C." The New Haven model, as shown in the 1881 catalogue, has a veneered case, making it similar to the Hamilton Clock

Company model. The cases of the Canada Clock Company II wall clocks were unveneered and made of stained butternut. The only other wall clock offered by the Canada Clock Company II was the "Regulator" model. As was often the case, the term "regulator," was used rather loosely, since the clock contained a standard movement. The design of the case, however, appears to be unique. No other illustration or actual clock by any American company was found to possess this exact shape. The clock combines a round bezel, a rounded lower case and a small circular glass door which is hinged. At first glance, it resembles the Japanese wall clocks that have been imported into North America in large quantities in recent years. (For an illustration of the Canada Clock Company "Regulator," see Fig. 43 and Fig. 160.)

To conclude this chapter, it can be said that the three companies appear to have made an honest effort to provide clocks that met contemporary standards of style, finish and value. Their designs were attractive and their workmanship good. Whatever the cause of their business failure may have been, the quality of their clocks, per se, does not seem to have been a major weakness.

Fig. 44 "M.E. Marks — Ottawa"
Hamilton Clock Company.

CHAPTER EIGHT
OTHER CHARACTERISTICS

In this chapter, some of the other distinguishing features — such as tablets, pendulums, trademarks, stamps and labels — of the Canada Clock Company I, the Hamilton Clock Company and the Canada Clock Company II are discussed.

TABLETS

Canada Clock Company I, Whitby

Any discussion of tablets used by the Whitby company must, of necessity, be short. The only clock that was made in any quantity during this period was the 30-hour ogee. The glass tablets that have been examined were found to be either mirrors or coloured tablets in a variety of designs. It has been difficult to judge whether these tablets were original to the clock or were later replacements. The only comment that can be made is that the tablets examined bore a close resemblance to contemporary American tablets. A variety of decorative designs exists and includes floral patterns, black and gilt scenes and conventional transfers. Overall, there seems to be no common characteristic. Any definite assessment is made difficult by the possibility of later restoration and the small number of clocks that survive.

Hamilton Clock Company, Hamilton

As noted before, when the company began operations at its new site in Hamilton, a much wider range of products was offered. A common characteristic of all these clocks was the widespread use of etched glass tablets. These tablets are found in all of the different models of clocks, including ogees, cottage, mantel and wall clocks. The use of etched glass tablets was also continued by the Canada Clock Company II after 1881. During this period, the City of Hamilton was the site of two major glass manufacturing concerns, the Hamilton Glass Company and the Burlington Glass Company. Although there are no specific records, it is reasonable to assume that one or both of these companies may have been the supplier of these tablets. It has been documented that the Burlington Glass Company was skilled in the etching of glass, using both acid and sandblasting techniques.

In any event, a wide variety of etched glass tablets exists. Illustrations of many of the tablets can be seen in Chapter 10. The patterns in the etched tablets are often geometric or floral. However, there are interesting variants in the tablets of clocks made by the Hamilton Clock Company. A number of tablets exists with religious themes, for instance, "Cling to the Cross," "Consider the Lilies," and "God Speed the Plough." One tablet has a French inscription, "Je reçois pour donner." One small cottage clock has the name of a jeweller etched on its glass, "M.E. Marks — Ottawa."

Most of the tablets are etched on one side only, but in the case of a tablet with the inscription "God Speed the Plough," etching was done on both sides of the glass, creating a three-dimensional effect. Although clear glass was generally used, one example is known of mirror glass with a pattern etched on the front surface.

Fig. 45 Etched Mirror Tablet
Hamilton Clock Company.

Although most of the tablets on Hamilton Clock Company clocks are etched, in a few instances silk screen or coloured transfer tablets have been found. Many of the non-etched tablets depict animal and bird scenes. A metallic sheen is sometimes present in the figures.

Canada Clock Company II, Hamilton

As noted above, the Canada Clock Company II also made wide use of etched tablets. However, they also used a variety of other decorative glass. Most of these designs resemble a silk screen technique, sometimes with the addition of hand colouring. The descriptive article in the *Canadian Manufacturer* on 19 October 1883, makes the following comment: "Many of the doors are handsomely stained and ornamented from designs gotten up in the factory, some of them also being hand-painted." The silk screen designs may have been homemade, but they were done in a very professional manner. It is interesting to note that, on some tablets, the Canada Clock Company II logo has been worked into the design. (see Fig. 46) The practice of depicting animals and birds, particularly on ogee tablets, was continued by Canada Clock Company II. Many of these glasses are quite handsome and have a metallic lustre.

The tablets used by both the Hamilton Clock Company and the Canada Clock Company II are quite distinctive. They appear to be of local origin and certainly do not resemble tablets found on any clocks of other manufacturers. The considerable variety of tablets can be seen from the illustrations in Chapter 10.

Fig. 46 Logo on Glass — Canada Clock Company II.

Fig. 47 This unusual "Sun and Moon" tablet was used occasionally by Canada Clock Company II.

PENDULUMS

Only ogee clocks have been documented as being made by the Canada Clock Company I in Whitby. Therefore, the story of pendulum bobs at Whitby is quite short. Existing clocks are equipped with typical ogee bobs made of cast lead with a sheet brass front. The diameters of the bobs in the clocks vary from 1½ inches to 1¾ inches. It is impossible at this point to determine how many of these bobs are original to the clocks. Similar lead bobs were used by the Hamilton Clock Company and Canada Clock Company II for ogee clocks and certain small mantel clocks. These bobs are similar, averaging 1½ inches in diameter. A larger bob of this type is found in the 8-day wall clocks, the bob being 2½ inches in diameter.

Fig. 48 Simulated Mercury Pendulums in three sizes were
used by Hamilton Clock Company and Canada Clock Company II.

Among the more elaborate mantel clocks, at least two distinctive types of pendulums were used. These were complete pendulums rather than simple bobs. The best known of these pendulums is a simulated mercury pendulum with a nickel-plated central "reservoir" and one brass bar on either side. These pendulums are found widely distributed in clocks of both the Hamilton Clock Company and the Canada Clock Company II. The pendulums are of three different lengths. The shortest was generally found in a time and alarm movement, the middle length in the 30-hour time and strike movement, and the longest in the 8-day time and strike movement. The lengths of these pendulums average 5½ inches, 6¾ inches and 7½ inches respectively. The size of the "reservoir" varies with each pendulum size. In addition, the larger pendulums are more decorative.

The other frequently occurring pendulum has a nickel-plated bob 2¼ inches in diameter, plus two imitation compensating rods made of brass. At the bottom of these compensating rods are two decorative leaves having some resemblance to maple leaves. A somewhat similar pendulum was made in the United States. However, there are minor differences in the contour of the lower nickel-plated bob.

Another pendulum style is illustrated in Fig. 50. This pendulum has been found in several clocks made by Canada Clock Company II. While not common, the authors feel that it is probably original.

76

Fig. 49 Round "Maple Leaf" Pendulum
frequently used by Canada Clock Company II.

Fig. 50 This pendulum has been seen in four
or five clocks by the Canada Clock
Company II and may be original.

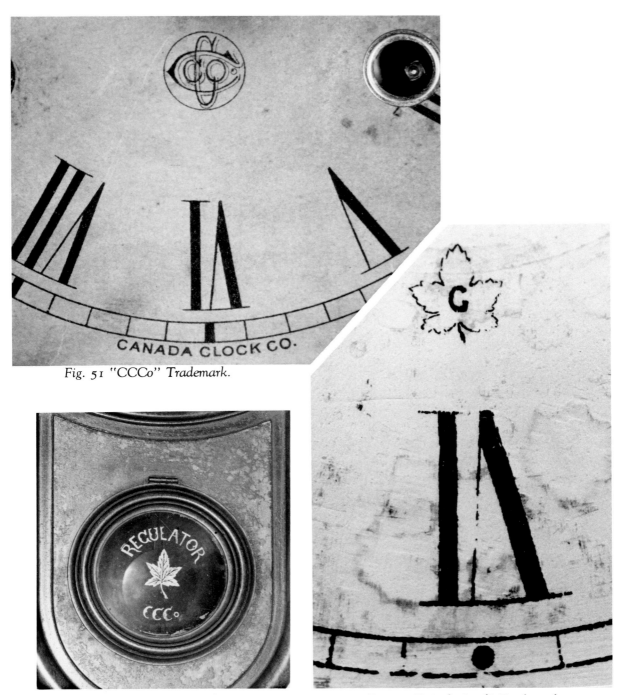

Fig. 51 "CCCo" Trademark.

Fig. 52 "CCCo" logo used on the "Regulator."

Fig. 53 "Maple Leaf" Trademark.

TRADEMARKS

No characteristic trademarks can be attributed to the Canada Clock Company I or to the Hamilton Clock Company. However, during the four-year period of clock manufacture by the Canada Clock Company II, a few simple trademarks evolved. One consisted of a concentric logo made up of the initials "CCCo." The other was a tiny maple leaf with the letter "C" enclosed within it. These logos are seen in clocks pictured in Fig. 51 and Fig. 53.

Fig. 54 Canada Clock Co. I Stamp.

Fig. 55 Hamilton Clock Co. Stamp.

Fig. 56 Canada Clock Co. II Stamp.

MOVEMENT STAMPS

Movements were stamped with the maker's name by each of the three companies. However, in each period, the practice seems to have been rather casual. In Whitby, of course, only one style of movement was made. From the limited number of clocks that the authors have examined, perhaps two thirds of the movements were stamped with a simple inscription, "Canada Clock Co." The Ansonia movements imported by Colonel Wallace were usually unstamped or occasionally marked with the Ansonia name.

A new stamp was used by the Hamilton Clock Company, stating "Hamilton Clock Co. Hamilton Ont." The stamp required a clear space 1½ inches in length and, therefore, was not used on small 30-hour time only movements. It was used fairly regularly, however, on the ogee movement and the two time and strike movements.

Under the Canada Clock Company II, the practice of stamping movements seemed almost to stop. Only a very few examples are known and are found mostly on 8-day time and strike movements. The stamp gave the name of the company — "Canada Clock Co." and differed from the stamp used at Whitby.

SOUNDING THE HOURS

The strike mechanisms of all three companies were quite simple and followed American trends of the period. Two basic sound sources were used — bells or helical gongs. Similar bells were used by the Hamilton Clock Company and the Canada Clock Company II. These were brass, usually nickel-plated. The bell used by the Hamilton Clock Company was 2¾ inches in diameter. The Canada Clock Company II used a bell 2½ inches in diameter.

Simple helical gongs were used in ogee clocks of the three companies. Similar gongs are found in cottage and mantel clocks with 30-hour time and strike movements. A more elaborate heavy steel, flat wire, coiled edgewise, was used in conjunction with a sounding disc in some of the more expensive mantel clocks produced by the Canada Clock Company II. On the gong sounding disc is the information "G.W. & A.C. Sanford — Patnd May 30, Dec. 5, 1882." George W. Sanford and Aaron C. Sanford, of Connecticut, patented their clock bell — patent no. 258609 — on 30 May 1882. The reissued letters patent, no. 10253, was issued on 5 December 1882. (Courtesy Horological Data Bank, National Association of Watch and Clock Collectors Museum Inc.) They described the gong as giving, when struck, "a clear tone of low pitch ... which will be prolonged with beautiful effect." The description quoted in Chapter 1 (*The Canadian Manufacturer*, 1883) refers to this gong and compares it to "some far off cathedral clock."

Small cast iron bells were used in clocks equipped with alarm mechanisms.

KEYS

Clocks and their keys become separated more often than not, so any comment must be very tentative. However, one style of cast iron key has been found with many Canada Clock Company II clocks. This key is illustrated in Fig. 57 with the observation that it "might" be original. Interestingly enough, the same key is found with the "Wanzer" mechanical lamp, which was also manufactured in Hamilton during the late 1880s. Thus, there may have been a local source.

Fig. 57 Key found with many Canada Clock Company II clocks.

LABELS

The labels are found inside the case for ogee clocks, but may be either inside the case or on the back of the case for spring-driven clocks. The characteristics of the variants for each company are discussed below.

Canada Clock Company I, Whitby
There are four known labels used by the Canada Clock Company I.

A. "No name" label. This label has been so named because no address or company officers are listed. One ogee clock has been found with a sales date of January 1875. This date confirms that it was used at Whitby. On the label, the engraved beaver faces left. This is probably the first label to be used by the company, because it is associated with the oldest form of ogee movement.

Fig. 58 "No Name" Label.

Fig. 59 "Greenwood-Collins" Label.

B. On the second label, the beaver faces right. The town is identified as Whitby and the company officers are identified as "J. Hamer Greenwood President" and "John F. Collins Manager."

C. The third label is identical to the second except that the name of "James Wallace Proprietor" has been substituted for "Greenwood."

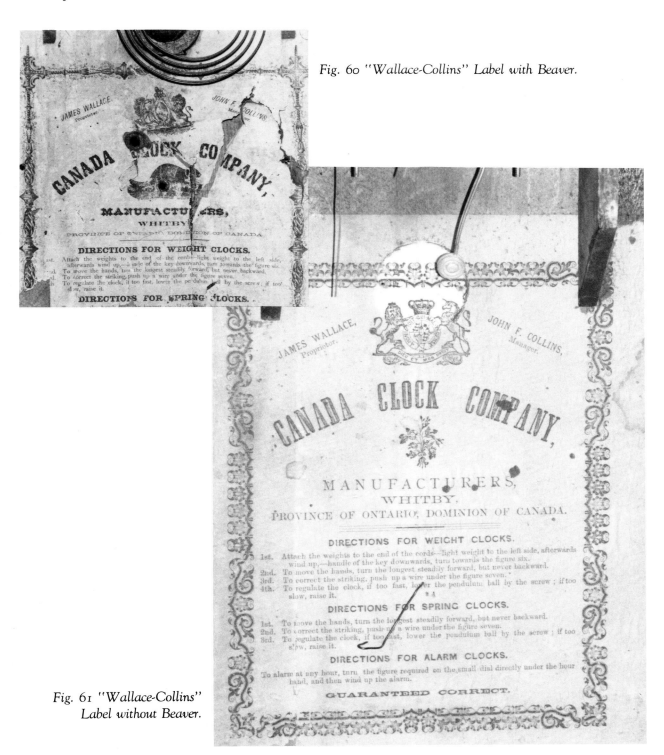

Fig. 60 "Wallace-Collins" Label with Beaver.

Fig. 61 "Wallace-Collins"
Label without Beaver.

D. The fourth label is an entirely different printing. There is no beaver present and the names of "James Wallace Proprietor" and "John F. Collins Manager" appear. The label is always associated with clocks containing an Ansonia movement, the last clocks made. None of these labels contains any information on the printer.

Hamilton Clock Company, Hamilton

A. Ogee label — two variants of the ogee label are known. The differences are small, however.

1. In the first label, the names of the three officers are given, namely "James Simpson President, George Lee Business Manager and J.F. Collins Mechanical Supt." This label shows a very clear engraving of the factory, measuring 4 3/8 inches by 3¼ inches and plainly marked "Hamilton Clock Company." Below, the company is given as "Hamilton Clock Company, Manufacturers, Hamilton, Ont." The printer is "Times Printing Company, Hamilton, Ont."

Fig. 62 Hamilton Clock Company, Ogee Label.

2. A second ogee label is identical to the label described above, but the names of Simpson and Collins are omitted. Only the name of "George Lee Business Manager" appears.

B. Labels of spring-driven clocks

1. 30-hour, time only — this small label, measuring 3¾ inches by 2¼ inches contains very little information and no printer's name. The company is given as the "Hamilton Clock Company."

Fig. 63 Small Label Hamilton Clock Company, for Cottage Clocks.

2. 30-hour, time and alarm label. Only one specimen of this label has been observed. The company is given as the "Hamilton Clock Manufacturing Company" and the names of the three company officers are shown.

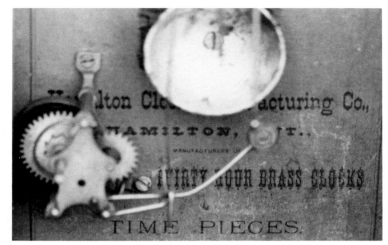

Fig. 64 Label in Time and Alarm Cottage Clocks.

Fig. 65 Outside Labels.

3. Mantel Clocks — outside label.

Two variants of this label are known and they are always located on the back of the clock. The labels are printed with either "1 day strike spring" or "8 day strike spring." The label includes a smaller and different engraving of the clock factory, measuring 2 inches by 1½ inches. The company name appears as the "Hamilton Clock Manufacturing Company." No officers' names are given. The printer is the "Times Printing Company, Hamilton, Ontario." The labels measure 6 inches by 3¾ inches and are printed in blue. This label is also found on the back of the octagonal wall clock.

4. Mantel Clock — inside label

This label is found in approximately 50 percent of all 30-hour and 8-day time and strike mantel clocks. There is no apparent reason for using this label instead of the preceding one. This label is always mounted inside the case, below the movement. It includes more printed information and is decorated with the small engraving of the factory described above. On this label, the company is called the "Hamilton Clock Manufacturing Co'y" and the names of all three company officers are shown. It is interesting to note that these clocks are described as being suitable for "locomotives." Since all clocks had pendulum escapements, they were obviously not suitable for a moving locomotive. Perhaps it can be assumed that the company was trying to obtain business with the railway station trade. It may also have been a rather unimaginative attempt to copy information that appeared on some American labels of the time.

Fig. 66 Inside Label.

5. Black and Gold Labels

These are found occasionally in 8-day mantel clocks. Printing is gold on black paper. The label is placed flat on the inside bottom of the case. The names of Simpson and Lee only are given and the printer was "The Times Printing Company."

Fig. 67 Black & Gold Inside Label.

Fig. 68 The "Simpson."

6. Labels for Specific Models

The only known named model manufactured by the Hamilton Clock Company is a time piece called "Simpson."

Canada Clock Company II, Hamilton

This company had the widest range of clocks, so it was not surprising to find that they had a wide variety of labels as well.

A. Ogee Labels

There are at least two variants of the ogee label. Both variants include a large engraving of the factory similar to that used previously by the Hamilton Clock Company, except that the name of the company in the engraving has been changed to "Canada Clock Company." Elsewhere on the label, this company was called the "Canada Clock Co'y (Limited), Hamilton, Ontario." The main difference in the two label variants is the decorative edge forming the border of the label. The printer is the "Spectator Printing Company," Hamilton.

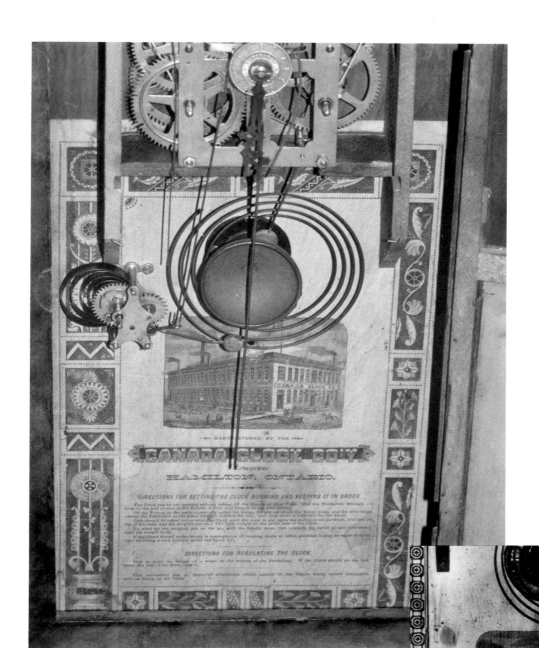

Fig. 69 Canada Clock Company II, Ogee Label, Type 1.

Fig. 70 Canada Clock Company II, Ogee Label, Type 2.

B. Spring Clock Labels

1. Stamped Labels

A major change in company identification was the use of an ink stamp on the back board of some of the spring-driven clocks. The maker's name and address and the clock model name were stamped on the back with a rubber stamp. This rubber stamping seems to have been used on most of the models at one time or another. The authors do not know whether this was an early or late practice. Certainly it was more economical than having labels printed. Although red ink was sometimes used for the imprint, a deep purple or black colour is more frequently found.

Fig. 71 *Typical Label Stamp, Canada Clock Company II.*

Fig. 72 *Stamped label "Tilley." This clock was named after Sir Leonard Tilley, the Father of Confederation and Minister of Finance in Sir John A. Macdonald's government of the 1880s. Tilley implemented the "National Policy" which gave the Canada Clock Company II a 35 percent tariff protection against imported clocks. He was the only Canadian politician to have a clock named in his honour. (Also see Fig. 140)*

Fig. 73 *Cottage Clock Label — Small.*

2. Cottage Clock Label — Small

This label is found in the small 9½ inch cottage clocks. It is a simple label measuring 5 inches square. There is no printer's name.

Fig. 75 This label is found on the back of a few mantel clocks. (Spectator Printing Company)

Fig. 74 Cottage Clock Label — Large.

3. Cottage Clock Label — Large

The large 12 inch cottage clocks have a very similar label to their smaller counterparts. The label size in this case is 6 inches square. The company is named, in both instances, "Canada Clock Company Limited, Hamilton, Ontario." The only additional information on the large cottage clock label instructs that the hands can be turned backwards without causing damage. This information appears to be unnecessary because the label was associated with time only movements, where the turning back of hands would not have been a problem in any event.

Fig. 76 Black and Gold Label.

4. Black and Gold Label

These labels were printed in gold on black paper and were installed below the movements inside the back of the clock. They were not widely used but can be found in some "City of Paris" models and the "City of London" model. The printer was the "Times Printing Company" Hamilton. The label dimensions are 4½ inches by 5¾ inches. The label states that hands can be turned back without injury even though it also states that the clock is time only.

5. Wall Clock Label

One label from a drop octagon wall clock has been examined and found to be different from other labels. There is an overall resemblance to the labels found in ogee clocks of this period. Central in the label is the large engraving of the factory and the print that was used is exactly the same as that found in the ogee labels. Much less information is included. The "Spectator Printing Company" printed this label. Anyone from Hamilton will be quick to point out that, undoubtedly, this is the same *Spectator* that, one hundred years later, continues to be Hamilton's daily newspaper.

Fig. 77 Octagonal Wall Clock Label.

Fig. 78 Specific Label for "Winnipeg."

6. Labels for Specific Clock Models

Perhaps the most interesting labels are those which the Canada Clock Company II had printed for specific lines of clocks. They were all printed by the "Times Printing Company" and appear to have been printed in different lots, because the type varies from clock model to clock model. The labels were used on both simple and elaborate clocks. Labels have been seen for the following models: Ontario, Winnipeg, Forest Beauty, Metropolitan, Crown Jewel, Niagara, Prince of Wales, Victoria and Golden Light. No doubt others exist.

Fig. 79 Specific Label for "Ontario."

Fig. 80 Specific Label for "Crown Jewel."

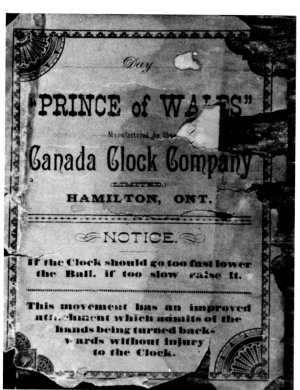

Fig. 81 This "Prince of Wales" label has been pasted over a smaller Canada Clock Company II label.

This discussion on the labelling practices of the three companies may well be incomplete. There seem to have been many short production runs and many changes of direction during the 12 or 13 years of the companies' existence. It is interesting to note that the first two companies were happy to declare the names of their company officers, but this practice was discontinued by Canada Clock Company II. This company, instead, began to give specific names to its various clock models. Someone used imagination in choosing names for these clocks. Many of the models were named after Canadian cities, towns and rivers. Others had more fanciful names. Collectors of clocks made years later by the Arthur Pequegnat Company of Berlin and Kitchener have noted with pleasure the fact that many of their clocks were named after Canadian town and cities. Credit for originating the idea, however, must be given to the Canada Clock Company II of Hamilton.

CHAPTER NINE
OTHER COMPANIES USING THE NAME "CANADA CLOCK COMPANY"

In addition to the two companies which operated in the nineteenth century and which are discussed in the previous chapters, two more companies used the trade name "Canada Clock Company."

On 9 May 1916, the "Canada Clock Company, Limited" of Toronto was established by five persons in the City of Toronto. These persons were: Ernest M. Dillon, Harold R. Frost and Henry E. Grosch, barristers-at-law; Ray T. Birks, student-at-law; and, Mona B. Banks, stenographer.

When the principals of the company applied to the Secretary of State of Canada for "letters patent" incorporating the Canada Clock Company Limited, one of the objectives was: "To buy, sell, manufacture, import or otherwise deal in clocks, time pieces, electrical master clocks, electrical clock systems, electric motor and programme attachments for the same and secondary and labor-saving devices of any kind whatsoever in relation to electrical clock systems, mechanical devices, including mechanical toys and electrical and other machinery and watches and jewellery of all kinds and any part or parts of the same."

The capital stock of the company was $250,000 divided into 25,000 shares of ten dollars each. Ernest Dillon, Harold Frost and Ray Birks were first and provisional directors of the company. No names of stockholders were given.

The company apparently didn't become a working company, as no mention of the company appears in the Toronto city directories in 1916 or in subsequent years.

The name "Canada Clock Company" was used again, however, and appears in the Toronto directories from 1926 to 1967. These records show Mr. George E. Bond as the manager, and the company locations were given as follows: In the 1920s, it was situated at 80 King Street E., Toronto; in the 1930s it had moved to 254 Adelaide Street W.; in the 1940s and 1950s, its address was at several locations on Wellington Street E.; and in the 1960s it was on Front Street.

Mr. Bond was the Canadian agent of the Synchronome Master Clock. This was an extremely accurate regulator used in factories and schools, etc. The Master Clock was driven by electrical impulses.

Fig. 82 Earliest Whitby 30-hour ogee "no name" label and earliest movement. Case inscribed "Sold to Wm. Rowland Jan. 20 1875."

PART IV
PICTURE PRESENTATION

CHAPTER TEN

CLOCKS MANUFACTURED BY
THE CANADA CLOCK COMPANY, WHITBY

Fig. 83 "Greenwood-Collins" label and second movement variation.

Fig. 84 Clock in Whitby Museum — same label as Fig. 59. Note that the tablet has the same design as Fig. 82.

Fig. 85 *"Wallace-Collins" label (with beaver) and second movement variant. Clock in the Centennial Building, Whitby.*

Fig. 86 *Last production at Whitby. "Wallace-Collins" label, (no beaver), Ansonia movement, no veneer on curved portion of the case.*

Fig. 87 *Second example of final Whitby production. Case has been stripped, showing absence of veneer on ogee curve.*

Fig. 88 *The only known mantel clock made at Whitby. Spring-driven Ansonia movement and ogee-type face.*

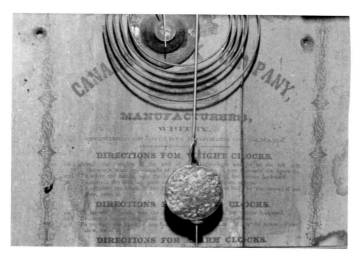

Fig. 89 *Label in above clock — "Wallace-Collins."*

CLOCKS MANUFACTURED BY
THE HAMILTON CLOCK COMPANY

Fig. 90 A group of clocks made by the Hamilton Clock Company and displayed at the May 1984 meeting of Canadian Chapters of the National Association of Watch and Clock Collectors.

Fig. 92 Religious themes in etched glass were common.

Fig. 91 Typical 30-hour ogee by Hamilton Clock Company. Animal tablet.

Fig. 93 *Labels in clocks Fig. 91 and Fig. 92 show names of Simpson, Lee and Collins. This clock gives Lee only.*

Fig. 94 *Small cottage clock by Hamilton Clock Company. Height 9½ inches.*

Fig. 95 *Larger cottage clock. Height 11¾ inches.*

Fig. 96 This clock is made in the so-called "Octagon Prize" case style and is the smaller of the two sizes. Height 16¼ inches.

Fig. 97 Three "Octagon Prize" type clocks with 30-hour and 8-day movements. Height 16¼ inches.

Fig. 98 30-hour time and strike clock. Note flat dial and the etched "Regulator" tablet.

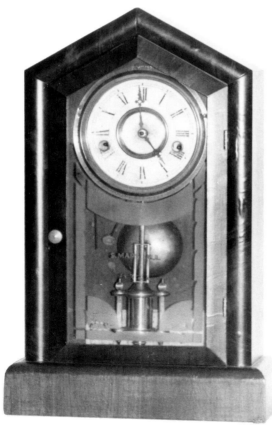

Fig. 99 30-hour striking clock with circular dial pan. Fig. 98 and Fig. 99 illustrate the use of wide and narrow moulding to form the case. Both clocks have the single-curve base.

Fig. 100 Square-topped mantel clock, 30-hour, striking.

Fig. 101 8-day striking clock. Fig. 100 and Fig. 101 show how a variety of cases were made from a single moulding. These clocks have the double-curve base. Two mouldings and two bases were used to make most of the Hamilton Clock Company's mantel clocks.

Fig. 102 Larger "Octagon Prize" type case with 8-day striking movement. Height 18½ inches.

Fig. 103 Another 8-day striking clock, again showing variation in case detail. Height 18 inches.

Fig. 104 *Miniature steeple clock, time only, made of solid tiger maple. This clock is very rare.*

Fig. 105 *This regular-sized steeple clock stands 19¼ inches high. 8-day striking movement.*

Fig. 106 *Regular steeple with 30-hour striking movement. Note again the use of standardized base and side moulding. The Hamilton Clock Company made the only true Canadian steeple clocks. Very few survive.*

Fig. 107 The Hamilton Clock Company
made a few clocks with high-quality, hand-
carved, solid walnut cases. Regular 8-day
striking movement. Small glass panels are
set into sides of case. Height 25½ inches.

Fig. 108 A second example of the high-
quality walnut clock. This clock has a
different base and minor variations in
carving.

Fig. 109 Octagonal wall clock by Hamilton Clock Company. Usually found with 8-day time and strike movement. Also quite rare.

Fig. 110 The "Simpson." This unique little 30-hour timepiece is the only clock by Hamilton Clock Company to have been given a name. (Named after Hamilton Clock President James Simpson.) Height 11¾ inches.

CLOCKS MANUFACTURED BY
THE CANADA CLOCK COMPANY LTD., HAMILTON

Fig. 111 Typical 30-hour ogee by Canada Clock Company II. This example has retained its original imitation woodgrain finish.

Fig. 112 Tablet detail. This is an excellent example of the use of animal motif. The figure is brightly coloured, with a metallic lustre. Case has been stripped, exposing solid butternut construction.

Fig. 113 Bird motif in Canada Clock Company II ogee. The unusual beaded moulding used to form the door can be seen clearly.

Fig. 114 "Montreal Cottage" 30-hour timepieces. Note minor differences in case and movement mounting. Left clock has slant-mounted movement.

Fig. 115 "Metropolitan Cottage" 30-hour time only movement.

Fig. 116 Second example of "Metropolitan Cottage," with noticeable differences in design. Both clocks are labelled.

Fig. 117 "Gem Cottage" 30-hour time and alarm clock. It has also been reported with 30-hour time only movement.

Fig. 118 "Hamilton Time" 30-hour cottage clock. This example was originally fitted with a separate alarm.

Fig. 119 'Montefiori" 30-hour time and strike.

Fig. 120 *Unnamed 30-hour time and strike by Canada Clock Company II.*

Fig. 121 *"Hamilton Cottage Extra" 30-hour time and strike by Canada Clock Company II. This clock is a variant of Fig. 118.*

Fig. 122 "City of Paris" 30-hour time and alarm. This case style is found in two sizes. Height 15¾ inches. Also found with time only movement.

Fig. 123 Larger version of Fig. 122 — "City of Paris" 30-hour time and strike. Height 19¼ inches. Also found with time only movement.

Fig. 124 "City of Paris" Junior and Senior.

Fig. 125 "Quebec" 30-hour time and strike.

Fig. 126 "Pembina" 30-hour time and strike.
The nickel-plated decorative ring on the dial
is fairly common on clocks by Canada Clock
Company II.

Fig. 127 "St. Lawrence" 30-hour time and strike.

Fig. 128 This clock closely resembles Fig. 127 and may be a variant.

Fig. 129 "Winnipeg" mantel clock, 30-hour time and strike — resembles New Haven "Neva" model.

Fig. 130 "Winnipeg" mantel clock showing significant differences from Fig. 129. This case would have been easier and less costly to produce.

Fig. 131 "Windsor" 30-hour striking mantel clock. This clock retains its original light finish on butternut.

Fig. 132 "Windsor" clock with 8-day time and strike movement.

Fig. 133 "Windsor" clocks were also offered as "Windsor Extra" (right). The difference was the addition of painted trim.

Fig. 134 "Hero" 30-hour time and strike mantel clock — bears a family resemblance to the "Windsor." (See Fig. 133) "Hero Extra" has also been identified and, like the "Windsor Extra," has painted trim.

116

Fig. 135 "Forest Beauty" 30-hour striking mantel clock.

Fig. 136 Two more "Forest Beauties." Many minor variations can be found in these clocks. In fact, no two seem to be identical.

Fig. 137 "City of London" model. This example is fitted with a 30-hour time and alarm movement.

Fig. 138 This "City of London" has the 30-hour time only movement and minor differences in decoration.

Fig. 139 "Niagara" mantel clock with 8-day striking movement.

Fig. 140 The "Tilley" model. 30-hour striking mantel clock in walnut.

Fig. 141 8-day time, strike and alarm version of preceding clock.

Fig. 142 8-day time and strike clock. Model name not known.

Fig. 144 Large mantel clock. 8-day time and strike. Model name not known. The clock has oval windows on each side. Height 22½ inches.

Fig. 143 "Crown Jewel" 8-day striking clock.

Fig. 145 This attractive hanging walnut clock resembles the "Ontario" model in many details. It is fitted with a 8-day striking movement and is quite rare.

Fig. 146 Second example of hanging clock has some minor variations in fittings and finials.

Fig. 147 "Golden Light" 8-day striking clock with side mirrors.

Fig. 148 This clock may be a variant of the "Golden Light." It has been fitted with a smaller dial and door.

Fig. 149 "City of Halifax" 8-day strike
mantel clock, fitted with metal cupid
statuettes.

Fig. 150 "Ontario" mantel clock with 8-day
time and strike movement. Part of the base is
missing.

Fig. 151 "Prince of Wales" 8-day time and
strike clock.

Fig. 152 *The name of this attractive clock has not been established. Usually seen with 8-day striking movement.*

Fig. 153 "Victoria" mantel clock, usually fitted with 8-day striking movement. Two styles are known. The decorated panel under the door is actually the front of a small drawer which can be pulled out to hold the key — an unusual feature.

Fig. 154 "Victoria" in second style. No drawer. It has a different pendulum and Sanford Patent chime. This was the most elaborate clock offered by Canada Clock Company II. Height 22½ inches.

Fig. 155 Octagonal wall clock with 8-day time only movement. Face bears the name of James Johnston, a jeweller in Whitby. Nevertheless, this clock was made in Hamilton by Canada Clock Company II.

Fig. 156 Octagonal wall clock with 8-day time and calendar movement. The opening at the dial centre seems to be solely for decoration. Movement is illustrated in Fig. 31.

Fig. 157 Second variant of calendar dial.

Fig. 158 *Wall clock with time, strike and calendar movement.*

Fig. 159 *Rare transitional clock. Case and label by Canada Clock Company II. 8-day time, strike and calendar movement by Hamilton Clock Company. Dial is a replacement.*

Fig. 160 *"Regulator" wall clock — a distinctive design by Canada Clock Company II.*

PART V
GENEALOGY

CHAPTER ELEVEN

OTHER CHILDREN OF ROBERT AND SARAH COLLINS

Robert (b. 7 March 1847, d. 9 November 1920) was born in Ireland, became a bookbinder and went to Minneapolis, Minnesota, where he lived for over 40 years. He was married at one time, but apparently had no children. He spent the last six years of his life at the Hennepin County Farm, Hopkins, Minnesota. He died of pneumonia and long-standing arteriosclerosis and heart problems. He is buried in Crystal Lake Cemetery, Minneapolis.

Frank Skelton (b. 25 May 1862, d. 19 September 1937) was born while the family was living in Guelph. In 1887, Frank married Maimee Adelaid (Dolly) Kerwin (b. 1865, d. 15 May 1944). Frank was a commercial artist and sign painter. He was also well known as a painter of landscapes. He spent some years in Hamilton with his brother Edward, who was also a painter, before going to New York to study art. When he returned he went to Toronto, where he lived for the remainder of his life. Frank was known as a "lightning artist" and won recognition for his speedy painting of pictures. When he was hired by a Toronto retail store, he painted 100 panels per day. He also gained a reputation as a painter of scenic effects for theatre stage settings. His son recalls that his father was frequently involved in stage shows given in Loew's Theatre in Toronto and, in one instance, he painted a panel of 12 feet by 8 feet, showing Niagara Falls, in 7 minutes. For many years Frank conducted a studio instructing many pupils in his "lightning" methods of painting. He is buried in Park Lawn Cemetery, Toronto, Ontario.

Eliza, Mary Ann and Alice. Although no accurate dates of birth are known for two daughters of Robert and Sarah, they were born in the period from 1854 to 1859. One girl, Mary Ann (b. 24 December, 1855, d. 30 May 1940) married Charles Mulligan and moved to Evanston, Illinois. Alice moved to Bermuda as the wife of Mr. Frank Bullin. Eliza died at an early age.

CHILDREN OF FRANK S. AND MAIMEE (DOLLY) COLLINS

Robert Kerwin, Adeline (married Alan Ince, son Robert K. Ince), William R., Frank (died of pneumonia), Isobel (d. 1922, was married to a Mr. Madden, daughter), Edward John (m. Ruth I. Smith, four children: Amaryllis R.C. married P. Blaiklock; Frank E.F.; Carol P. married R. Wiens; John R.).

CHILDREN OF J.H. AND CHARLOTTE GREENWOOD

Mary Harriet (b. 5 May 1866) became superintendent of the Jewish Hospital at Cincinnati, Ohio.

Charlotte Jane (b. 11 January 1868).

Thomas Hubbard (Viscount Hamar) (b. 7 February 1870, d. 10 September 1948). The *Oshawa Times* characterized him as "Whitby's most famous son."

Thomas H. Greenwood was baptized Thomas Hubbard Greenwood and in his youth was known as Tom. He graduated from the Whitby Model School and taught for a short time in the public school in Manchester, Ontario. After serving for a time in the militia, he attended the University of Toronto, graduating in 1895. While at university he took part in a students' strike, resulting in changes in the operations of the university. Among the strikers were W.L. Mackenzie King and Arthur Meighen who both became Prime Ministers of Canada.

Tom was an ambitious man and he felt that England was the country where his ambitions could be fulfilled. According to Reverend Canon E. Ralph Adye, Tom wished to be a bencher in Gray's Inn, to enter Parliament, to gain a peerage and to be married in Westminster Abbey. Tom went to England in 1895, changed his name to Hamar and worked his way through college by lecturing on temperance. The income from these lectures, however, was not sufficient to see him through the legal training he wanted, and he supplemented his income from a settlement he received from a bus company for an accident in which he was thrown from a bus and nearly killed. He became a bencher in Gray's Inn, as well as treasurer of that law society.

In 1906, Hamar Greenwood entered British Parliament as a Liberal for York riding and became parliamentary secretary to Winston Churchill. In 1911, he married Marjory Spencer, daughter of Walter Spencer of Townhope Court, Hertfordshire, England. The wedding ceremony took place at Westminster Abbey. In 1913, he wrote a book about Canadian life and government. Its title was *Canada as an Imperial Factor*. In 1915, his last ambition, that of obtaining peerage, was finally fulfilled. He was honoured by King George, who conferred upon him a baronetcy. In 1937, he was "created first Viscount Greenwood of Llanbister" for his many assignments in the military and in Ireland. The eldest of his two sons, David Henry Hamar, born in 1914, succeeded to the title. In 1938, the honourary degree of Doctor of Law was conferred upon him by the University of Toronto.

His wife was appointed C.B.E. in 1920 and advanced to D.B.E. in 1922 for her services in Ireland.

Viscount Hamar Greenwood died in London in 1948 and the funeral services were held at Westminster Abbey, St. Margaret Chapel.

On the 100th anniversary of his birth, the Whitby Historical Society displayed their collection of photographs and other documents pertaining to Hamar, Viscount Greenwood. A special memorial service was held in All Saints Anglican Church, Whitby, where a stained glass window was dedicated in memory of his parents.

William H. (b. 11 January 1872) became managing editor of the *Toronto World*.

Isabella R. (b. 3 February 1874).

Arthur H. (b. 3 August 1877).

Adeliza Florence (b. 20 August 1879) married Leopold C.M. Stennent Amery (b. 22 November 1873, d. 1948), and they had two sons. Amery was born in India and was a friend of Sir Winston Churchill. Their friendship began when they were schoolmates at Harrow. A mischievous event occurred when Amery, only 5 feet tall and a senior at Harrow, was pushed into the swimming pool by Churchill, who was in the lowest form of the school. Amery retaliated by holding Churchill under the water fully clothed until he cried for mercy.

Amery had a distinguished career in the British Public Service. The highlights of his career are summarized below: became a member of the British Parliament in 1911; fought in the War of 1914; was appointed to the personal staff of the Secretary of State for War; was appointed Parliamentary Under-Secretary of State for the Colonies in 1919; appointed Secretary of State for the Colonies from 1924 to 1929; appointed British Secretary of State for India and Burma in 1940.

In spite of his busy career, he found time to write eleven books. Among them was the seven volume *Times History of the War in South Africa*.

In November 1942, after the German occupation of France, a number of persons started to broadcast from Berlin asking the British to stop the war against Germany. The most active was William Joyce, the notorious Lord Haw Haw, who was an American with a British passport. He was eventually tried for treason and hanged. During this period, a man who insisted that he was John Amery, the son of Leopold Amery, began broadcasting from Berlin asking the British to stop the war against Hitler and blaming the "Jews and Communists for the crimes against civilization." His father, who had not heard from John since he went to France to nurse a lung affliction, announced that "the voice did not sound like my son's nor did the material. I have nothing more to say."

Oliver Rosebrough C. (b. 16 August 1881).

Margery V. (b. 22 February 1883).

Gladys C. (b. 2 October 1886) (Mrs. Simon Rodney).

CHILDREN OF ADAM RUTHERFORD

From his first marriage Adam had seven children. Four daughters lived to adulthood. (Family tree is available from J. Varkaris.)

Jane (Jennie) (b. 3. July 1872, d. 14 February 1940) married Lieut. Col. W.R. Turnbull, sons William Lester Turnbull and John Rutherford Turnbull.

Margaret E. (b. 23 March 1874, d. 17 May 1960), married Henry E. Murdock, no children.

Sarah L. (died as an infant in 1876).

Thomasine (b. 22 September 1877, d. 7 October 1968) married John James Hobson, five children: John Adam, Sarah Katharine, Richard Musson, Thomas Patrick, Blanche Rutherford.

Blanche S. (b. 28 October 1879, d. 6 October 1963) married C.T. Beatty.

Infant (d. 1884).

Nelles Rutherford (b. 1898, d. 1960) was the son of Adam Rutherford and Maria. He married Marjorie Harris and, after serving in World War I, lived in the old Nelles Manor in Grimsby.

CHILDREN OF JAMES AND MARION SIMPSON

James Jr. (b. 1856, d. 1927) worked for his father as bookkeeper in Simpson, Stuart and Company, Hamilton. Around 1884, James Jr. formed a partnership with his father. After a short stay in Buffalo, New York, about 1901, James Jr. returned to Hamilton and made it his home. He is buried in Hamilton Cemetery.

Agnes (b. about 1860) married R.S. McIndoe and lived in Toronto.

Archie T. (b. 1866, d. 1921) was an actor more familiarly known by his stage name of Andrew Robson. Archie lived in New York City, but died in Los Angeles. He is buried in the Hamilton Cemetery.

Robert Russel (b. 1869, d. 1940) was a hotel proprietor. In 1901, he was associated with Cataract House, Niagara Falls, N.Y. By 1907, he was proprietor of Hotel Royal in Hamilton. Also, he was president of the Hamilton Jockey Club for many years. Robert Russel married Jessie Saunders (b. 1873, d. 1951). She was a regent of St. Elizabeth Chapter, Toronto, of the I.O.D.E. She and her husband are buried in Hamilton Cemetery.

Edward S. lived in Gold Run, Yukon Territory in 1901 and in Dawson City in 1907.

CHILDREN OF ROBERT RUSSEL AND JESSIE SIMPSON

Thomas Edward (b. 1903, d. 1912) is buried in the family plot in Hamilton Cemetery.

Jessie Eleanor (b. 1914, d. 1947) married John Edward A. Hyslop of Hamilton. She was active in sports and was a devoted member of Westdale United Church. There were three children: Suzanne, Carol and Brian.

Marion Gertrude married first Thomas Hislop of Toronto, and later Arthur D. Meridith of Toronto.

CHILDREN OF JAMES AND ELSPETH WALLACE

William (b. 8 October 1846, d. 19 October 1937) was a school teacher, a prospector and a saw mill owner. He travelled extensively across Canada, United States and Mexico. In 1905, he was in Knee Hill Valley, B.C. He lived in Vancouver when that city was a village called Coal Harbour and taught school in the Kootenay District when the transcontinental railway had just been completed. However, his fondest memories were of Ontario County. "Travel was by the old Welland line between York and Whitby, each tollgate charging a penny. Trade was in barter. Every store boasted a barrel of whisky at the end of the counter where the customer had a drink on the house. The now dormant Whitby harbour was once a hive of industry. I have seen wagons of farmers lined up for over two miles waiting their turn to unload. Horse racing took place on the ice." He is buried in Union Cemetery, Oshawa. His wife, Mary Grant Wallace (b. 1863, d. 24 September 1937), is buried by his side.

Two daughters of James and Elspeth Wallace are buried in Rosehill Cemetery, Chicago.

Mary Wallace (b. 1847, d. 15 May 1889) lived with parents.

Annie (b. 1853, d. 3 April 1905) lived with parents. The youngest daughter, she took care of her mother. Annie died after contracting rheumatic fever.

James Jr. (b. 1851, d. 1893).

Little is known of a third daughter who married Alexander M. McLaren of Chicago.

APPENDIX 1

CLEARING SALE AT THE CLOCK FACTORY, WHITBY

The subscriber being anxious to close his business with the least possible delay, begs to intimate that he will on Wednesday the 19th day of July, 1876 offer for sale by public auction, without reserve, at the Factory, Brock Street, the following valuable property, viz:

500 30 hour O. G. Weight strike Clocks, in beautiful and highly finished cases, warrented.

100 8-day "Octagon Prize" spring strike, do. do.

120 30-hour do. do. do.

85 30-hour and 8-day Cottage do. do.

3 Highly finished Clocks, 8-day strike weight.

20 Regulators with fine movements. The greater part of the clock movements have been imported from the celebrated "Ansonia Clock Company" Connecticut, and can be thoroughly relied upon as time keepers.

6 dozen Picture and Looking Glass frames, small, large and veneered.

200 Ladies' Work Boxes, veneered in Rosewood, Mahogany and Satinwood.

1 dozen Ladies' Shawl and Lace boxes, veneered Size 2f 2in x 1f 3in — 6in deep.

1 dozen Knife and Spoon boxes, same size.

6 Crystal Lamps with Hangers and Reflectors.

1 large Wall Show Case, glass front.

A quantity of Tools, various useful for carpenters or cabinet makers.

A quantity of Mahogany veneers, and partially finished wood work for Clocks, Work Boxes, etc.

3 Carpenter's Benches, 1 Cabinet Maker's bench, 1 Circular Saw Table, 1 heavy seat for turning lathe 7 feet long, with a number of other articles connected with the factory.

Also the remains of a stock purchased in England, consisting of Jet and Gold Jewellery in Pins Brooches, Ear-rings, Finger rings, Bracelets, Cuff Buttons, Studs, etc. 24 boxes of Sewing Machine attachments suitable for a majority of the machines now in use with a number of other useful articles.

The quantity of goods being large, the sale will commence at 11 a.m. sharp, and will continue in the evening.

The clocks will be sold singly or in lots, to suit purchasers.

TERMS CASH

L. FAIRBANKS
Auctioneer

JAMES WALLACE

N.B. The Subscriber may state that all who can and who have the ready should attend this sale, as many years may pass before another such opportunity to get bargains may present itself.

APPENDIX 2

WHITBY CHRONICLE, May 24, 1877
CLOCKS, CLOCKS, CLOCKS

"The Canada Clock Company, having decided to close their business here will for three weeks only, offer the following valuable stock of clocks at manufacturer's prices. Therefore parties wishing to get a first-rate clock at a very low price for a short time have a very good opportunity.

The movements are of the best class and have been imported from the United States and put into cases of Whitby manufacture which for style and finish are superior to any in the country.

The stock comprises Eight Day and 30 hour Octagon Prize Spring Strike Clocks, Eight Day and 30 hour Cottage Spring Clocks, Eight Day Calendar Spring Strike Clocks, Eight Day Calendar (large), Hall and Dining Room Clocks, Weight Strike, Regular 8-day Clocks. All are warranted to measure time exactly.

There will also be offered a quantity of work and knife boxes (veneered), picture frames (veneered), a cabinetmaker's bench, a quantity of veneers and a number of articles in the way of clock trimmings and tools."

APPENDIX 3

From CANADA GAZETTE, Vol. VII, No. 6, Saturday, August 9, 1873
APPLICATION FOR CHARTER BY LETTERS PATENT

Notice is hereby given that the persons whose names, addresses and callings are hereinafter mentioned intend to apply, after the expiration of one month from the first publication hereof in the Canada Gazette, to his Excellency the Governor General in Council for a Charter of Incorporation by Letters Patent, under the great Seal of the Dominion of Canada, under the Provisions of the Act passed by the Parliament of the Dominion of Canada, in the thirty second year of Her Majesty's reign, Chapter thirteen, entitled "The Canada Joint Stock Companies Letters Patent Act, October, 1869."

1. The proposed corporate name of the Company is "The Canada Clock Company (Limited)."

2. The object for which incorporation is sought is the Manufacture and sale of clocks, timepieces and watches of all kinds and descriptions.

3. The operations of the proposed Company are to be carried on at the town of Port Hope, in the County of Durham, in the Province of Ontario and said Dominion.

4. The amount of the capital stock of the Company is $50,000.

5. The number of shares is 500 and the amount of each share is $100.

6. The names in full and the addresses and callings of the applicants are as follows:

William Barron Butterfield, Gentleman
Arthur Trefusis Steneage Williams, Member of the Provincial Parliament
James Guest Williams, Gentleman
all of the said town of Port Hope, and
William Fitzpatrick Collins of the town of Whitby in the County of Ontario and said Province of Ontario, Clock Manufacturer and said persons whose names and addresses and callings are specially mentioned as above, and who are all subjects of Her Majesty by birth or naturalization, are to be the first Directors of the said Company.

Dated at Port Hope this 5th day of August A.D. 1873
Smart & Smith, Solicitors for applicant.

(Authors' Note: Arthur Trefusis Steneage Williams was a well-known personality in Port Hope. He was a politician, soldier and member of a wealthy family. He achieved fame and notoriety during the Riel Rebellion and the Battle of Batoche in 1885. During the battle, he disobeyed orders and mounted a bayonet charge at a time when the Métis were running out of ammunition. Many Métis were slain, the battle won and Riel later captured. Williams was hailed as the "Hero of Batoche" but died shortly afterwards before he could reap his hero's reward or face court martial.

SOURCES OF INFORMATION

The Public Archives of Ontario
The Public Archives of Canada
The National Library of Canada
Vital Statistics Records of U.S.A. and Canada
The New Brunswick Museum
The Whitby Museum
Whitby Public Library
Illinois State Historical Library
Hamilton Public Library
Thomas Fisher Rare Book Library, University of Toronto
Toronto Trust Cemeteries
Union Cemetery, City of Oshawa
Forest Hill Cemetery Company, Chicago
Waterloo Historical Society
Whitby Historical Society

BIBLIOGRAPHY

Bailey, T.M. "Dictionary of Hamilton Biography." Hamilton, 1981.
Beers, L.H. & Co. "Illustrated Historical Atlas of the County of Ontario," Toronto, 1877.
Burrows, G.E. "Canadian Clocks and Clockmakers," Oshawa, 1973.
Farewell, J.E. "County of Ontario," Whitby, 1907.
Johnson, L.A. "History of the County of Ontario," Whitby, 1973.
Mackay, R.W.S. "Hochelaga Dipicta," 1846.
Morgan, E.P. & Harvey, F.L. "Hamilton and Its Industries," Hamilton, 1884.
Plewes, J. "Repairing and Restoring Pendulum Clocks," New York City, 1984.
Taylor, S. "The Noble Jerome Patent 30-hr. Brass Weight Movement and related movements,"
Bulletin of the National Association of Watch and Clock Collectors Inc., Vol. XXIV, No. 6, Part II,
Dec. 1982.
Winter, B. "A Town Called Whitby," Whitby, 1967.
Varkaris, J. & C. "The Pequegnat Story: the Family and the Clocks," Dubuque, 1982.
Presbyterian Church, Whitby, "As All Our Fathers Were, 1833-1975."

OTHER SOURCES:
Canadian Illustrated News; Current Biography, 1942; The Canadian Manufacturer; The Trader;
The Canada Gazette; Proceedings of the Council of Whitby; Ontario Living magazine, November
1985, "Soldier's Quarters" by M. Byers and M. McBurney; The Mercantile Agency Reference
Book, July 1884, Dun Wiman & Co.

LIST OF ILLUSTRATIONS

INDEX